Occupational Therapy 20·00

25.1- 88.

Joint Protection and Rehabilitation in Chronic Rheumatic Disorders

Joint Protection and Rehabilitation in Chronic Rheumatic Disorders

New revised enlarged edition

Merete Brattström, MD

Wolfe Medical Publications Ltd

Copyright © Merete Brattström 1973, revised edition 1980, 1987

Published in Sweden as 'Ledskydd och Rehabilitering vid
Inflammatorisk Ledsjukdom', © Studentlitteratur ab, Lund, Sweden

English language version published by Wolfe Medical
Publications Ltd, 1987 ©

Printed by Butler and Tanner Ltd,
Frome, Somerset, England

ISBN 0 7234 0907 2

CONTENTS

FOREWORD TO THE SECOND EDITION

Merete Brattström

Since the publication of the first edition of this book, developments in rheumatology and rehabilitation have proceeded apace, so that it has become necessary to revise and enlarge the original material.

The present book is principally intended for use by doctors, ergotherapists, physiotherapists, nursing staff and social workers, as an aid in the treatment and rehabilitation of patients suffering from chronic polyarthritis. I try to show that there is rarely a single factor which can lead to an improvement in the patient's situation. Treatment must be seen as a complex interaction of various medical, surgical, social and psychological measures over a long, drawn-out disease process. The object of all these efforts must be to meet the needs of the patient at home, at work, and during leisure hours. Working in a team is necessary to correlate these efforts.

The first section describes the physical problems encountered in chronic arthritis and gives brief details on evaluation of the disease process. To those interested in acquiring a deeper knowledge of such matters, I would recommend the standard works on anatomy and rheumatology, which would also lead to a better understanding of the various diagrams. A discussion of the functional activities carried out in everyday life, the requirements of the patient vis-à-vis his or her home and place of work, and a discussion of psychological reactions to a chronic disease conclude the first section of the book.

In addition to contracture prophylaxis and adapting to a new way of life, joint protection also covers the numerous technical aids and implements available, as well as more specialised aids such as orthoses. Suitable measures which can be taken to help with the cervical spine, the upper extremities, the back and the lower extremities are described in separate chapters, and the importance of exercising the muscles is discussed. In addition to all these forms of joint protection, there are various changes and adaptations which can be made in the home. The special problems that confront mothers suffering from rheumatism are dealt with, as well as the difficulties experienced at work, and the possible impairment of sexual function.

This is followed by a section devoted to patient education. A schematic summary of the aims and possibilities of treatment at various levels of function concludes the second section.

In the illustrated section, various situations in daily life are shown in which the joints could easily suffer damage as a result of incorrectly applied forces. These illustrations show the right and the wrong way to approach various tasks. They can be used by the patients themselves, or serve to illustrate instruction given by a therapist, possibly in conjunction with slide presentations and the patient instruction sheets 1–6.

The present book is the result of intensive collaboration between doctors, physiotherapists, ergotherapists, social workers, nursing staff and secretaries at the University Rheumatological Outpatients Centre in Lund.

Brigitta Althoff, Håkan Brattström, Ido Leden, Lennart Mannerfelt, Ulrich Moritz, Ulla Nordenskiöld and Jan Pahle have contributed much valuable advice to help the project along. Göran Sunden checked the anatomical details and David Haffajee checked through the chapter on the hand and types of orthosis available, providing a useful commentary and supplying some of the drawings. The remaining graphics were provided by Ingemar Nilsson. My thanks are due to Gunilla Kilenstam, Barbro Gierow and Inta Selga for their painstaking work in editing. Ingrid Jönsson drew up the bibliography.

This greatly revised and extended edition of '*Joint Protection*' has been influenced to a considerable degree by Kåre Berglund's ideas on ways to 'humanise' the care of patients. I have derived much help and inspiration from all the patients I have come to know over the years and for whose understanding of the problems and of the disease I have the greatest respect. I thank them all from the bottom of my heart.

I owe a special debt of gratitude to Dr. Wilhelm Martin Zinn, Medical Director and Chief Physician of the Medical Department at Bad Ragaz and at the Intercantonal Rheumatism and Rehabilitation Clinic, Valens, Switzerland, as well as his staff, for their work in translating this book and publishing the second edition in German.

And finally my thanks go to Anne Chamberlain, who kindly and with great competence read the English version, and the translators who rendered the German edition into English.

Lund, 1987

PART I

THE PRINCIPAL CHRONIC INFLAMMATORY DISEASES OF THE JOINTS

Chronic polyarthritis

Chronic polyarthritis and rheumatoid arthritis are inflammatory diseases affecting the joints and occurring in approximately 1.5% of our population. The disease can be observed in all age groups, but above all in the middle age groups. Women account for three times as many patients as men. In the age group 50-55 years, ca. 7% of all women, but only 3% of all men, are affected (Allander 1970).

The actual causes of chronic polyarthritis are not known. It is not certain whether a virus, or bacteria or other substances produced by the body itself are initiating and maintaining factors in the rheumatoid process. Nevertheless, many of those affected are carriers of an as yet undetermined tissue antigen closely correlated with the so-called HLA-DR4 group.

The changes which have the greatest effect on the body functions are those which take place in the joints, where the synovial tissue lining the inside of the joints is enlarged and becomes heavily vascularised. This tissue contains many cells (granulocytes, lymphocytes, monocytes, plasma cells) which are typical of chronic inflammatory processes. These cells produce a series of harmful enzymes, while the plasma cells produce mainly certain proteins, the immunoglobulins IgG, IgA, IgM, including the so-called rheumatism factors. The joint cavity is considerably extended as a result of overproduction of synovial fluid, which also contains white blood cells and various enzymes which attack the joint cartilage and other tissue. The thickened synovial membrane increases greatly in size and grows, generally along the blood vessels, underneath or even into the joint cartilage. The cartilage is broken down ('digested') and in time it can be undermined by bone absorption. The synovial tissue can also grow out along the ligaments, in the knee for example, around the cruciate ligament or even around the menisci, and thus contribute to the destruction of these structures. The diseased synovial tissue has sometimes been compared with a snail which eats its way into the top of a mushroom. (The hollowing out of the bony

11

substance looks rather like the snail's shell.) On an X-ray, the loss of bone tissue stands out clearly as erosions.

Similarly thick synovial tissue rich in blood vessels can be found at the tendon sheaths, especially in the hands and feet, but it can also be found in the form of nodules in the vicinity of the tendons on palpation of the flexing tendons of the fingers. Tenosynovitides occur as a result of increased friction between tendons and tendon sheaths and can lead to restriction of mobility. The invasion of rheumatic tissue which grows between the individual fibres of the tendons can also weaken the tendon, and finally lead to rupture. Rubbing against sharp edges of bone is also a frequent cause of ruptures of the flexor and extensor tendons of the fingers (see p. 45)

The inflammatory reaction of the rheumatic disease can affect the entire connective tissue. Under the skin, one can frequently see or feel the so-called rheumatic nodules, said to be found in areas which are frequently subjected to pressure, such as the elbows and the hands. However, they can also be found on other parts of the body, such as the cranium. Diffuse changes in the connective tissue and even rheumatic nodules can also occur in the lungs. In about 10% of cases, rheumatic inflammation can also be found in the pericardium, in the form of pericarditis. Frequently the eye is also affected by uveitis and scleritis (Hazleman and Watson 1977). The blood vessels can be attacked in different ways. Not so rarely, the inflammatory vascular obstructions can lead to severe histological lesions such as ulcers, especially on the legs or, if the blood supply to the peripheral nerves is impaired, these nerves can be damaged, sensory and motor nerves being affected in different degrees right up to polyneuropathy. These manifestations of rheumatic disease occur when it moves into a malignant phase which is difficult to check.

Ankylosing spondylitis (Bechterew's disease)

Ankylosing (or rheumatoid) spondylitis is a chronic form of arthritis whose aetiology is likewise not fully explained but which, like other seronegative chronic polyarthritides, is associated with the presence of the tissue antigen of the HLA-B27 group in the cells of the affected patient (Brewerton *et al.* 1973). The terms seropositive and seronegative merely refer to the occurrence and identification of the rheumatoid factors in the serum of the patient. With ankylosing spondylitis, the inflammatory process as a rule attacks the sacro-iliac joints, the small joints of the spine and the joints between the ribs and the thoracic vertebrae first of all. There is a pronounced tendency to ankylosis due to ossification of the ligaments of the spine and because the joint capsules become fibrous. The peripheral joints frequently become involved, for example, in 60% of all cases diagnosed, the hip joints and/or shoulder joints, the acromioclavicular joints and other joints, especially the large ones, were found to be affected (Moll 1980). In juveniles, the disease not infrequently manifests itself first as arthritis in one or both knee joints.

The manifest disease is considerably more frequent in men than in women, in contrast to chronic polyarthritis. Previously, one assumed a ratio of 4–9:1. However, in large-scale examinations among the population, in which inactive and clinically quiescent cases are also recorded, as well as cases which had not previously been diagnosed, a ratio of only 5:3 in favour of men was found, at an overall incidence rate of 1% of the entire population for morbid changes. The first symptoms of the disease are usually observed between the ages of 15 and 25, but frequently, the correct diagnosis is not made until later. The disease can, in a small percentage of cases, lead to considerable functional disturbances, especially if the peripheral joints are affected, such as the shoulder joints, hips and knees, or when the spine stiffens in a pronounced kyphotic or kyphoscoliotic posture.

In ankylosing spondylitis too, extra-articular complications can arise on occasions. Valvular heart disease can occur, with inflammation and fibrosis, or recurrent inflammation of the iris (iridocyclitis) can affect the patient's vision. Various authors assume that infections of the urinary passages or intestines could play a part in the aetiology of this disorder.

Juvenile chronic polyarthritis

Arthritides which occur before the conclusion of a patient's 15th year come under the definition of juvenile chronic polyarthritis. It may occur in only a few joints, generally affecting the peripheral joints first, and then symmetrically. It can, however, occur in only a few joints, but asymmetrically, generally in the knee, ankle and hip joints, as well as the odd finger joint.

When it occurs in a polyarticular form, internal organs are often affected as well, whereas in the other form (few joints, asymmetrical), the inflammatory process can affect the eyes, particularly in the form of iridocyclitis or anterior uveitis.

A detailed discussion of diseases of the joints is left to the appropriate standard works (Ansell 1980, Kelley *et al*. 1984).

FUNCTIONAL PROBLEMS WITH INFLAMMATORY DISEASES OF THE JOINTS

Pain

The inflammatory process, or synovitis, is always connected with pain when the corresponding joint is moved or subjected to a load. This inflammatory pain is always most pronounced in the morning. In addition to the pain, patients also mention the stiffness, which can last for several hours after waking. Highly active synovitides can even lead to pain when the joint is resting, especially in the large joints, such as the shoulder, hip and knee joints.

Back pain is particularly bad at night and in the early morning with spondylitis ossificans of the pelvis. Arthrosis pains, on the other hand, are felt particularly keenly at the beginning of a movement, and are therefore commonly known as starting pains. Quite a different pain is experienced if a nerve becomes compressed at a narrow point. An example of this is the median nerve in the carpal tunnel on the volar side of the wrist, where it can be compressed by the flexor tendons if the tendon sheaths are swollen with tenosynovitis. This pain is often burning in character, combined with paraesthesia, and occurs at night in particular (see 'The wrist', p. 42). Patients frequently describe it as 'like wax, burning on your hand'. Corresponding pain is experienced when the occipital nerve is compressed, if the small joints in the cervical spine are affected, or with instability in the atlanto-occipital joint, or in the region of the ulnar nerve in synovitis and capsulitis of the elbow joint. A further point at which a nerve can be exposed is where the medial popliteal nerve runs under the ligamentum laciniatum behind the medial malleolus.

In general, it can be said that pain leads to an increase in muscular tension as a reflex, and also to a weakness of the affected muscles. In addition, of course, pain affects the patient's psychological state.

Contracture

By contracture we mean the shortening of the muscles and shrinking of the connective tissue. A joint that is causing pain and is filled with fluid is generally kept in the position in which the joint cavity is at its largest and the capsule can best be relaxed to the fullest possible extent. This relieves the pain, but from a functional point of view, it is incorrect. In time, the activity of the synovitis falls off, and the connective tissue, which is rich in blood vessels, becomes fibrotic and shrinks. The result is contracture.

Mobility can be restricted on the one hand by changes in the joint itself, as for example in synovitis, through damage to the cartilage or the adjacent parts of the bone, and on the other hand by changes outside the joint, such as a fibrotic and shrunken capsule, shortening of the tendons and muscles or finally through other changes which take up extra space, such as cysts near the joint (Baker's cysts and others).

The risk of contracture is particularly high in ankylosing spondylitis and also in juvenile chronic polyarthritis.

Muscle weakness

Muscle weakness is a major problem in inflammatory diseases of the joints (Isenberg 1984). The synovitis and the pain lead to inhibition of muscle function, which is confirmed by electromyographic examination (Moritz 1976, 1977). This is of particular importance in the region of the quadriceps muscle, whose strength can be drastically reduced by pain caused by tension resulting from a capsule that is full to bursting with fluid. Consistent pain leads to inactivity and eventually to wasting of the muscles. The ability to activate and control the contractile element of the muscles, i.e. the motor units, is greatly reduced by the pain and the muscle contracture.

In a healthy muscle, we distinguish between two different types of muscle fibre: Type I consists of slowly contracting fibre, while Types IIA and IIB consist of rapidly contracting fibre (Saltin 1977). Recent research has shown that it is the rapidly contracting fibres of Type II that are damaged in particular by the inflammatory rheumatic process (Isenberg 1984).

The rheumatic disease can also lead to inflammatory foci in the muscles, i.e. to rheumatic inflammation of the muscles (myositis or polymyositis) (Moritz 1963). The muscles are also weakened by inflammation. If peripheral nerves are affected by the disease as well, then the effect on nerve conduction can also lead to paresis and muscle wasting. Electromyographic examination is the simplest aid to diagnosis of myositis in particular, or myopathy in general. Symptoms of weakness can also be caused mechanically, for example, by stenosing inflammation of the tendon sheaths in the hand or in deformities caused by damage to cartilage and bone. This is especially the case if the path of the muscle has been changed by damage of this sort and the muscle itself has become relatively too long or too short. The mutilating changes found in the wrist and the finger joints are an example of this telescoping phenomenon.

Instability

If joint cartilage and bone are destroyed by the rheumatic disease, not only the muscles but also the tendons become relatively too long, and the ligaments lose their stabilising effect. These changes in the biomechanical relationships are very often the cause of progressing deformities in the joints. This is clearly seen in the case of the knee joint. The changes which occur in chronic arthritis are as a rule particularly pronounced on the outside of the joint and result in a valgus position (see 'The knee joint', p 65). Instability in the region of the wrist and finger joints occurs particularly obviously where the mutilating changes in bone and cartilage mentioned above have occurred, or after destruction of the stabilising soft tissue apparatus.

EXAMINING PATIENTS WITH ARTHRITIS

Treatment of any inflammatory disease of the joints must be based on the most thorough examination of the medical, functional and psychosocial situation of the patient. Whatever the patient considers particularly important for his (or her) daily life, for the continuation of his occupation and for his leisure hours must serve as a guideline for the team involved in planning the treatment. It is patients who should determine in which areas they require help, and in what order.

Medical assessment

The activity of the disease

A chronic disease of the joints takes place in stages, i.e. there are differing levels of activity at different times. At times when the inflammatory activity is pronounced, the patient's condition can deteriorate very badly and rapidly whereas at low levels of activity, it can remain apparently stable for longer or shorter periods of time. The activity of the disease can be assessed in a number of ways.

Joint status

Joints with active synovitis are frequently painful to the touch, hot, and give rise to pain on movement. The number of active joints is an acceptable yardstick by which to measure the activity of the disease (with regard to mobility, see also 'Assessment of function', p. 20). (Ritchie 1968, Lansbury 1966.)

Morning stiffness

If the patient keeps notes on how long the morning stiffness lasts, it is possible for the doctor to form an accurate picture of the activity of the disease. A duration of more than 30 minutes is considered to be a significant symptom in diagnosis of chronic polyarthritis. In making this assessment, one must take into consideration any medicaments, especially those taken late at night.

Assessment of the pain

An analysis of the pain experienced is also an important aid to determining the activity of the disease. The patient's experience of pain can be quantified in numerical terms or in the form of a line on a graph (visual analogue scale of pain, the significance of which has again been debated in recent times). As a rule, the patient is perfectly capable of describing the level of pain (Huskisson 1976).

Strength of grasp

The strength of grasp of the hand can be measured with a vigorimeter (Mannerfelt 1966) or quite simply with a sphygmomanometer cuff. The strength of grasp will depend partly on the degree to which the wrist, the bottom and middle joints of the fingers, the tendons, nerves and muscles of the hand are affected by the disease, but also partly on the pain. If the disease is very active, then only a weak force will be registered because of the pain caused by the effort. The strength of the grasp is thus more a measure of the pain experienced than of the maximum strength the patient can bring to bear.

In synovitis of the knee joint too, the strength of the quadriceps can be increased not only by suitable exercises, but also by relieving the pain (Tiselius 1969). Measurement of the patient's strength can therefore vary considerably from day to day and from hour to hour in chronic polyarthritis.

Blood sedimentation

The composition of blood proteins is changed at high levels of inflammatory activity. This increases the blood sedimentation rate. Above all, the content of so-called acute phase protein fractions (C-reactive proteins), immunoglobulins, complement and fibrinogen can vary considerably, depending on the activity of the disease. The diagnostic value of the blood sedimentation rate should not be overestimated. There are examples of high sedimentation rates after the disease has been in progress for many years, without a correspondingly high rate of activity in the joint process. High sedimentation rates can also be caused by other diseases, for example, by infections, anaemia, tumours and amyloidosis.

Haemoglobin

As a rule, inflammation and especially inflammatory diseases of the joints can lead to anaemia, which cannot simply be ascribed to lack of iron. The reason lies rather in a disturbance of the processes for utilising the iron. In this respect, the severity of the anaemia does provide a yardstick for measuring the level of activity. During the course of the diseases, microscopic or even macroscopic haemorrhages may occur. The first occurs relatively frequently, as a result of taking certain drugs, for example, minor stomach haemorrhages caused by taking salicylate preparations. The cause of any anaemia must in any case be thoroughly investigated.

Rheumatoid factors
The rheumatoid factors belong to the immunoglobulins, i.e. they are auto-antibodies which can be found in the majority of patients with chronic polyarthritis. These are rarer in juvenile chronic polyarthritis, and are not found in ankylosing spondylitis. The causes of the formation of rheumatoid factors are still not clear but experience has shown that a positive test has a definite prognostic value.

Severity of the disease

It is extremely difficult to give long-term prognoses with chronic diseases of the joints. The acute occurrence of a highly active form occasionally gives rise to a relatively favourable prognosis, while a form which proceeds from the very onset in an insidious creeping manner can lead to severe invalidity. In most cases, it is the patients with the above-mentioned rheumatoid factors and rapid rates of erosion who have to face up to a particularly bad prognosis. By erosions we mean the signs of cartilage and bone destruction that show up on X-rays of the affected joints. The occurrence of rheumatic nodules and systemic manifestations in the blood vessels, organs, nerves, muscles and skin are also unfavourable factors from the point of view of a prognosis.

In assessing the degree of severity of the disease, continual observation is of particular importance. In order to be able to quantify accurately any improvements that may occur during the course of treatment, or any further deterioration, a number of different index systems have been proposed (Lansbury 1966, Ritchie *et al.* 1968, Lee *et al.* 1973, Smythe 1975).

Joint and muscle status

A detailed description of the methods used to measure mobility in the joints and muscular strength is beyond the scope of this book. For reasons of clarity, a certain amount of anatomical detail has been included here which can then be studied in greater detail, if required, with the aid of an anatomical atlas (American Academy of Ortho-paedic Surgeons).

Inspection: Swelling, reddening, deformity, nodules

Palpation: Painful to the touch, swollen capsule, exudation, over-heating, nodules

Function: Active mobility, passive mobility, functional mobility, possibly also pathological mobility, instability

The status of the joints can change, depending on the time of day and on the medication provided. It is therefore important that both the time of day and the medication should be noted down. When assessing muscle function, any atrophy found should be accurately described. Measurement of muscular strength is, as we have already said, a debatable point, since it is often a measure of the pain experienced in the process, rather than an indication of reduced innervation or muscular tone. Precise joint status with details of mobility of the joints and muscular functions form an important part of the functional examination. However, their real value is only realised when they are placed in the context of the patient's needs in everyday life.

Assessment of function

General remarks on function

Inflammation of the joints impairs the ability of the patient to match up to the requirements of day-to-day living and to follow his (or her) normal occupation. Much can be done to alleviate the situation, but in view of the number of different ways of pursuing this aim, it is sadly often possible to miss the best way. For this reason, it is advisable to classify the degree of functional impairment of the patient, so that an accurate and reproducible description of the patient's status is always available.

In accordance with the American Rheumatism Association (ARA), we distinguish between four classes of function (after Steinbrocker *et al.* 1949). Patients with functional capacity of Grade I can cope with daily life without any restrictions on their normal activities. Grade II implies a considerable reduction in functional capacity, but the patients generally manage without having to resort to technical aids. They can also continue with their normal occupa-tions, possibly with some slight adjustments, and generally have to put up with relatively few restrictions on their normal activities. Functional capacity Grade III implies that patients depend on technical aids and the assistance of helpers. Following an occupation is only possible to a very limited degree, if at all.

Patients with functional capacity Grade IV rely heavily on helpers to get them through their daily lives. They are as a rule confined to a wheelchair, or even bedridden.

The following table shows the results of research by Allander (1970), carried out in a large section of the population, into the classification of chronic polyarthritis sufferers by functional capacity. Approximately 15% of his cases fall in the two top categories, III and IV. The figures in the right-hand column come from the Rheumatism Outpatients Centre of the University of Lund, where for obvious reasons a large proportion of the patients come into the higher categories (Brattström 1970).

Classification of functional capacity after Steinbrocker in the large-scale investigation carried out by Allander and among the patients of Rheumatism Outpatients Centre of the University of Lund, in average values per 100 patients:

		Number of patients	
Grade	Degree of incapacity	Allander	Lund
I	Copes with daily life without any limitations	Not taken into account	
II	Capable of normal activities, possibly with minor adjustments, in spite of pain and some limitations on movements	87	38
III	Major difficulties, depends on others for help with dressing, hygiene, eating, and transport	11	45
IV	Completely dependent on others for help, completely or almost completely confined to wheelchair or bed	2	17
		100	100

We often see a patient managing to maintain a certain functional level for a considerable period of time, until something happens to start off a new phase in the disease, increasing the inflammatory process and further impairing the functional capacity of the patient. If one does not intervene quickly, there is a risk that the patient may drop into a lower grade. In such cases, it is most important to recognise the situation in good time. The fall from Grade II to Grade III means for most patients that they have to give up their job, thereby restricting their social contacts and removing an important incentive. It also means that they usually become dependent, at least partially, on some other person to help them to cope with some of the essential functions in their daily lives. A reasonably stable patient in Grade III who is dependent on help from others only to a limited extent can in risk situations very rapidly turn into a rheumatic patient completely confined to a wheelchair and entirely dependent on other people. At worst, if there was no way of caring for them at home, they would have to be taken into a hospital or special home. Both of these situations involve sweeping changes, both for the patient and for those entrusted with their care. Naturally, we must do everything possible to ensure that such situations do not arise.

Risk situations of the type mentioned above can arise in many ways, for instance, through infections, such as influenza or an infection of the urinary tract. Certain types of stress can also bring them on, and there is always risk after a fracture that necessitates immobilising the patient for a time, especially if the necessary facilities for physiotherapy are lacking. During pregnancy, disease activity usually decreases, but the process can soon start up again after birth, often coming in the form of very severe bouts of activity (Östenson 1983).

Sudden deterioration in the patient's condition can also have psychological causes, arising out of considerable difficulties in their personal life or some other misfortune. Finally, we should also mention that very hot baths, in which the patient gets over-heated, can also lead to increased inflammation. Awareness and avoidance of possible risk situations thus become important parts of the assessment and treatment of the chronic polyarthritic patient.

Measuring function

Quantitative measurement of functional ability is of great importance for assessment of the success or otherwise of the various treatments given. The rather sketchy classification described above provides only a rough and ready assessment of functional ability. The 'risk awareness' which we stress in our own approach, i.e. the constant awareness that things could suddenly change for the worse, coupled with a knowledge of the possible causes, represents a refinement of the constant observation approach required with chronic polyarthritis and allows it to be integrated into clinical practice. Classification by grades, however, is only a very coarse method of assessment, so lacking in graduation that it requires a relatively major change in circumstances, such as regaining the ability to walk after a total hip replacement or similar operation on the knee, for a patient to move up from Grade III to Grade II.

The literature contains a large number of so-called ATL indices. These are sets of tests drawn up to permit a more precise measurement and description of functional status. Most of them were developed in rehabilitation clinics, in order to be better able to determine the effects of treatment given there (Katz *et al.* 1963–70; Mahoney and Barthel, Maryland Disability Index 1965; Lee *et al.* 1973, Swezey 1978, Fries 1980, Liang 1981, Pincus 1983, Meenan 1980). In the ATL index drawn up by Katz *et al.*, the most varied activities are included, such as dressing, eating and drinking, taking a bath, visiting the toilet and getting around one's own home. A distinction is then made between three levels of function: fully functional, partially functional and completely dependent on help from others. By using this index system, one can differentiate between seven functional classes. Using the measuring system drawn up by Swezey (see p.25), one can differentiate between upper and lower extremities, and there are five levels of function. The index drawn up by Lee in 1973 (also shown on p.25) is suitable for simpler analysis of case histories. Here again, it takes account only of sizeable changes in functional ability.

The simple self administered questionnaires have proved to be valuable in clinical trials of medical treatment. Probably they will prove valuable also in clinical work with groups of patients, where it is important to follow changes and functional capacity as a whole, for instance in patients treated surgically.

The functional disability index questionnaire according to Fries, as shown overleaf, is an example. Evaluations of its validity, reliability, concision and coherence have been performed. The index is calculated by taking the highest score from each of the eight questions, adding them together and dividing the total by eight, and recording the patient's overall index on the scale of 0 to 3.

Disability index questionnaire after Fries

	0 without difficulty?	1 with difficulty?	2 with some help?	3 unable to do?
1. DRESSING AND GROOMING Are you able to:				
a. get your clothes out of the closet and drawers	–	–	–	–
b. dress yourself including handling of closures (buttons, zips, snaps)	–	–	–	–
c. shampoo your hair	–	–	–	–
2. ARISING Are you able to:				
a. stand up from a straight chair without using your arms for support	–	–	–	–
3. EATING Are you able to:				
a. cut your meat	–	–	–	–
b. lift a full cup or glass to your mouth	–	–	–	–
4 WALKING Are you able to:				
a. walk outdoors on flat ground	–	–	–	–
5. HYGIENE Are you able to:				
a. wash and dry your entire body	–	–	–	–
b. use the bathtub	–	–	–	–
c. turn taps on and off	–	–	–	–
d. get on and off the toilet	–	–	–	–
6. REACH Are you able to:				
a. comb your hair	–	–	–	–
b. reach and get down a 5 lb bag of sugar which is above your head	–	–	–	–
7. GRIP Are you able to:				
a. open push-button car doors	–	–	–	–
b. open jars which have been previously opened	–	–	–	–
c. use a pen or pencil	–	–	–	–
8. ACTIVITY Are you able to:				
a. drive a car (For reasons other than arthritis, I do not drive—)	–	–	–	–
b. run errands and shop	–	–	–	–

Assessment of function after Swezey

A. Upper extremities
Eating, personal hygiene, dressing and undressing, writing, telephoning.

B. Lower extremities
Locomotion, i.e. walking around indoors and outdoors, ascending and descending stairs, rising from a prone position to a sitting position and from a sitting position to a standing position. Getting into bed and getting out of bed. Taking a bath and using the toilet. Getting in and out of a car. Driving one's own car.

Degrees of severity

1. Normal	Patient can cope with anything without difficulty.
2. Independent	Patient manages everything, though with certain difficulties.
3. Partially independent	Patient needs help from others or special aids or special planning because of pain, weakness or limitations on mobility.
4. Partially dependent	Patient requires help from others for certain functions and requires aids.
5. Dependent	Patient requires help for most activities.

Assessment of function after Lee

1. Can the patient turn his head from one side to the other?
2. Can the patient comb the hair at the back of his neck himself?
3. Can the patient close a drawer with his hands?
4. Can the patient open doors unaided?
5. Can the patient lift a full pot of coffee?
6. Can the patient drink from a cup using only one hand?
7. Can the patient turn the key in the lock?
8. Can the patient cut meat with a knife?
9. Can the patient butter a slice of bread?
10. Can the patient wind a clock?
11. Can the patient walk?
12. Can the patient walk a. without someone to assist?
                    b. without a crutch?
                    c. without a stick?
13. Can the patient climb stairs?
14. Can the patient stand with knees straight?
15. Can the patient stand on tiptoe?
16. Can the patient bend low enough to be able to pick up an object from the floor?

The answers to these questions are coded as follows:
    0 = yes, without difficulty
    1 = yes, but with difficulty
    2 = no

The cervical spine

Anatomy and function

The human head weighs ca. 5–6 kg. It is held in place on the cervical spine, resting on the two atlanto-occipital joints, by means of the extremely powerful stabilising ligaments between the occiput and the first and second vertebrae and by the tone of the surrounding muscles. The two atlanto-occipital joints are coordinated and as a result of their anatomical arrangement, permit only a bending and stretching of the neck as a compromise movement. Between the first and second vertebrae there is a central joint which consists of two sections, a front section situated between the front arch of the first cervical vertebra and the anterior surface of the odontoid process of the second cervical vertebra, and a rear section between the cartilaginous joint surface resting on the transverse odontoid ligament and the posterior surface of the odontoid process of the second cervical vertebra, and two side joints. They are also closely connected with one another by means of the transverse ligament of the atlas. The odontoid process of the second cervical vertebra lies embedded like a cylindrical ring in the above-mentioned apparatus. The second vertebra is attached to the atlas and the occipital bone by means of the alar ligaments of Arnold (1).

The amount of movement between the first and second cervical vertebrae in the sagittal plane (extension and flexion of the head) roughly corresponds to that between the head and the first cervical vertebra and normally amounts to between 10° and 20°. The main movement that takes place between the atlas and the dens is rotation, of the order of approximately 30° to either side. However, there are very considerable differences between individuals in respect of this movement. The anatomical shape of the joints and the very powerful, inelastic ligaments permit almost no lateral flexion between head, first and second cervical vertebrae in a healthy person (Djian and Zinn 1959). The joints between occiput, first and second cervical vertebrae are in principle identical in structure to all the other joints, with cartilage, synovial membrane and capsule. The articulated connections between the body of the vertebrae of the middle and lower sections of the spine from C2 onwards correspond to the intervertebral disc joints of the thoracic and lumbar spine.

The articulated connections between the bodies of the vertebrae C2 to T1 permit, on average, approximately 10° of rotation to either side in each case, 10° extension/flexion in the sagittal plane and 3–5° lateral flexion to either side.

Muscles in the region of the head

Flexion – Rotation

At the front of the neck lie the muscles which flex the neck, superficially arranged on either side of the sternocleidomastoid muscle which has its origin at the mastoid process and its insertion at the sternum and clavicle. Somewhat lower down are the scalene muscles, which arise from the cervical vertebrae and are inserted into the 1 – 3 ribs. Deep down are the rectus capitis anterior muscle, the longus capitis muscle and the longus cervicis muscle. The sternocleidomastoid muscle on the one side turns the facial part of the skull to the opposite side when it contracts. When both sternocleidomastoid muscles are contracted together, the head is bent forwards.

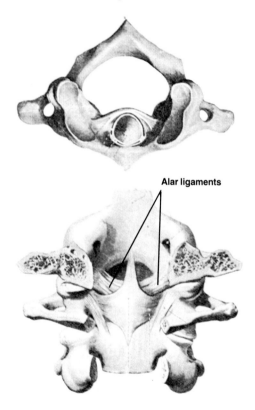

Alar ligaments

1 Cervical vertebra (atlas), seen from above (top). Lower picture: occiput, C1 and C2 together with their dorsal ligaments, seen from behind after removal of the arches and spines, and of the spinal cord and membranes.
After W. Spalteholz: Hand Atlas of Human Anatomy. Verlag Hirzel, 1904.

Extension – Rotation

Extension of the neck is the result of contraction of a large number of different muscles. Situated under the skin is the trapezius muscle which has its origin at the occiput, the ligamentum nuchae and the spinous processes of the cervical and thoracic spines and its insertion at the clavicle, the acromion and the spine of the scapula. Below the trapezius is a layer consisting of the splenius cervicis muscle, the semispinalis capitis muscle and the semispinalis cervicis muscle, while right at the bottom, the small, short neck muscles combine synergistically to form a powerful extensor muscle.

Lateral flexion of the neck is performed by synergistic interaction on the part of various muscles, controlled by the sternocleidomastoid muscle on the same side.

In the nape of the neck there are a number of structures which can cause painful changes. These are mainly muscles, blood vessels, peripheral nerves, connecting tissue in ligaments and intervertebral discs and the small posterior cervical joints. A detailed description of all the possible causes of pain in the neck would far exceed the bounds of this book.

Functional mobility

Juveniles and adults in middle age can normally bend and stretch the neck without experiencing any pain. The average total amplitude of movement in the sagittal plane usually amounts to about 100°, while the lateral flexion to either side is at least 40°.

The cervical spine in inflammatory diseases of the joints

In chronic arthritis, inflammatory changes occur in the joints of the cervical spine between the occiput and the first thoracic vertebra in 35 – 85% of cases of different patient groups. The cervical spine can be affected at all stages of the disease, and the intensity of the local process can often differ widely from the level of activity generally found in other localities (Martel 1961, Redlund Johnell 1984, Kaufman 1983, Smith *et al.* 1972).

In the course of synovitis in the joints between C1 and C2, the stabilising structures such as ligaments and muscles can be severely damaged and stretched. The resulting instability in the neck causes the atlas, together with the skull, to slide forward when bending the head, so that the odontoid process of C2 can be pressed against the spinal cord which runs behind it in the vertebral canal. In most cases, this amounts to a pathological mobility, in which the atlas can return to its normal position on extension of the head back into the middle position or into the extension position. However, fixed luxations in a forward position can occur (2 and 3).

The rheumatic granulation tissue can cause bone erosion at and under the joint surfaces and can also 'eat' the odontoid process of C2, or – in rare cases – even separate it from its body. As a result, the structures in the nape of the neck as a whole become shortened, so that the head and atlas come to rest lower down relative to C2, than they would in a healthy individual. One could refer to this as a downwards luxation.

The instability described can be seen very clearly on an X-ray. The most important view is from the side, with the head in maximal flexion. In a healthy individual, the maximum distance between the front arch of C1 and the odontoid process is 4 mm, both with the head in its normal position and also when in maximal flexion. Any greater distance suggests a pathological mobility or instability or a subluxation, depending on whether the enlarged gap reduces to a normal size again or not.

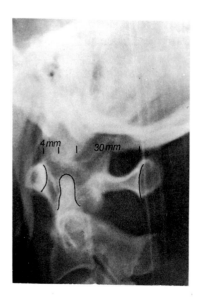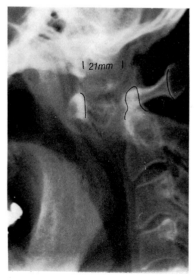

2 and 3   X-rays of a patient with pronounced instability of the atlanto-occipital joints: whereas in the upright position the distance between the rear joint surface of the front arch of C1 and the front joint surface of the spine is 4 mm, it increases to 21 mm when the head is bent.

The changes in the uppermost part of the odontoid process discussed above can lead in individual cases to compression of the spinal cord and corresponding tetraparesis. As a rule, these conditions first manifest themselves as tautness and vague paraesthesia in the arms, in attacks of cramp in the calf muscles in the night, spasticity and loss of muscular control in the legs and disorders of sensibility.

If the neck is affected in chronic polyarthritis, the resulting compression of the greater and lesser occipital nerves can lead to dorsal headaches which are difficult to treat. If the blood vessels are affected, i.e. the vertebral artery, this can manifest itself in cerebral symptoms and cause vascular headaches, dizziness and occasionally abasia.

Compression of the spinal cord can lead to tetraparesis, and in rare cases even to tetraplegia, which may require emergency surgery to relieve compression on the spinal cord (Brattström and Granholm 1976, Mikulowski et al. 1975, Mikulowski 1979). In this connection, the effects of relatively minor trauma can lead to the sudden death of a rheumatic patient, if the head is passively bent.

Instability with accompanying luxation can also occur in the other sections of the spine. Inflammatory spondylolisthesis can occasionally occur at several levels, which show up impressively on X-ray as step-shaped deformities. Instability and subluxations of this type can lead to peripheral radicular failure through compression of the nerve roots in the intervertebral foramina. As a result of the atrophy of the tissues and bone that often occurs to a considerable extent, compression of the cervical nerve roots and the spinal cord in the neck is fortunately rare at these levels. It is therefore possible for instability that appears quite marked on an X-ray not to give rise to any clinical symptoms. On the other hand, analysis of neurological abnormalities in patients with gross destruction and deformities can be notoriously difficult.

In ankylosing spondylitis, both the intervertebral disc connections and the small joints of the vertebrae are relatively frequently affected in the region of the cervical spine. The tendency to stiffness can be considerable, and in many cases it is impossible to prevent the neck stiffening up altogether. The possibilities for treatment are then principally restricted to attempting to ensure that the neck stiffens up with the head in an acceptable position relative to the thoracic cage.

The cervical spine is affected relatively frequently in juvenile chronic polyarthritis as well. The disease affects the growth processes here and can lead to ossification. Ankylosis of the bones also occurs. As a result of this, growth is interrupted, so that later on, when the patient has reached adult age, the affected vertebrae show up on X-ray as relatively small rectangles tilted upwards.

Upper extremities

Joints of the thoracic girdle

Anatomy and function

The thoracic girdle comprises the humeroscapular joint, the sterno-clavicular joint, the acromioclavicular joint and the articulated connections between the shoulder blade and thoracic cage.

The humeroscapular joint is a spheroid joint which permits the greatest possible degree of movement, due to a small joint surface on the scapula and a very wide capsule. The stability is, relatively speaking, correspondingly low, which is only compensated in part by the long biceps tendon and the powerful rotator muscles.

The shoulder blade is kept in its rest position by the relatively powerful muscular apparatus. Its enormous mobility greatly increases the radius of action of the arms and hands. If the upper arm is abducted as far as possible, for example, then only 90° of this movement is accounted for by the humeroscapular joint. The amount of movement in excess of 90° is made possible by the extremely flexible articulated connection between scapula and thorax (Cailliet 1967).

Movements of the shoulder joint
Lowering

Trapezius muscle	Extends from the occiput, the ligamentum nuchae, and the spines of the cervical and thoracic vertebrae to the clavicle, the acromion and the spine of the scapula.
Innervation:	Accessory nerve (C4).
Pectoralis major muscle	Extends from the clavicle, sternum and rib cartilage 1–6 and from the aponeurosis of the stomach muscles to the crest of the greater tuberosity of the humerus.
Innervation:	Ventral thoracic nerves (C5–C8).

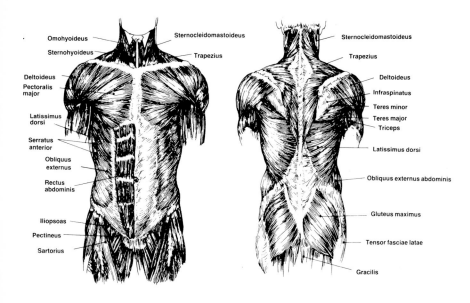

4   The external muscles of the trunk and the shoulder and pelvic girdles
After: J.G. Chusid and J.J.McDonald: Correlative Neuroanatomy & Functional
Neurology, Lange Medical Publications, 1967.

Latissimus dorsi muscle	Extends from the ribs 10–12, the spines T6–12, the fascia lumbodorsalis and the iliac crest to the crest of the lesser tuberosity of the humerus.
Innervation:	Nerve to latissimus dorsi muscle (thoracodorsal nerve) (C6–C8).

Forward movement of the shoulder blade

Serratus anterior muscle	Extends from the ribs 1–8 to the medial edge of the scapula.
Innervation:	Nerve to serratus anterior muscle (C5–C8).
Pectoralis major muscle	See above.

Backward movement of the shoulder

Trapezius muscle	See above.

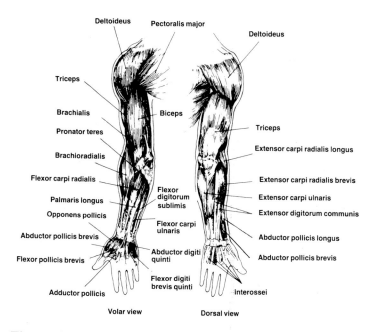

Deltoideus
Pectoralis major
Deltoideus
Triceps
Brachialis
Biceps
Pronator teres
Triceps
Brachioradialis
Extensor carpi radialis longus
Flexor carpi radialis
Extensor carpi radialis brevis
Palmaris longus
Flexor digitorum sublimis
Extensor carpi ulnaris
Opponens pollicis
Extensor digitorum communis
Flexor carpi ulnaris
Abductor pollicis brevis
Abductor pollicis longus
Flexor pollicis brevis
Abductor digiti quinti
Abductor pollicis brevis
Flexor digiti brevis quinti
Adductor pollicis
Interossei
Volar view
Dorsal view

5 The muscles of the arm
After: J.G. Chusid and J.J.McDonald: Correlative Neuroanatomy & Functional Neurology, Lange Medical Publications, 1967.

| Rhomboid muscles | Extend from the ligamentum nuchae, the spines C6–C7 and T1–T4 to the medial edge of both shoulder blades. |
| Innervation: | Nerve to the rhomboids (C3–C5). |

Raising the shoulder

Trapezius muscle	See above.
Rhomboid muscles	See above.
Levator scapulae muscle	Extends from the spines C1–C4 to the upper medial angle of the scapula.
Innervation:	Nerve to the rhomboids (C3–C5).
Pectoralis major muscle	See above.

Rotation of the lower angle of the shoulder blade upwards and outwards

Serratus anterior muscle   See above.

Trapezius muscle   See above.

Rotation of the shoulder blade towards the media and downwards

Rhomboid major muscle   See above.

Movements of the upper arm in the shoulder joint

Abduction

Deltoid muscle	Extends from the clavicle, the acromion and the spine of the scapula to the tuberculum deltoideum of the humerus.
Innervation:	Circumflex nerve (C5–C6).
Supraspinatus muscle	Extends from the supraspinous fossa of the shoulder blade to the greater tuberosity of the humerus.
Innervation:	Suprascapular nerve (C5–C6).

Movement forward/upward = flexion

Deltoid muscle	See above.
Parts of the pectoralis major muscle	See above.
Coracobrachialis muscle	Extends from the coracoid process to the crest of the lesser tuberosity of the humerus.
Innervation:	Musculocutaneus nerve (C6–C7).
Biceps brachii muscle	Extends with its long head from the upper edge of the joint surface of the shoulder blade and with its short head from the coracoid process to the proximal radius and attaches there to the tuberculum radii.

Innervation:	Musculocutaneus nerve (C6–C7)

Adduction of the upper arm

Latissimus dorsi muscle	See above.
Lower part of the pectoralis major muscle	See above.
Triceps brachii muscle	Extends from the infraglenoid tubercle of the shoulder blade over the rear side of the humerus and attaches with two heads to the olecranon.
Innervation:	Radial nerve (C6–C7–C8).
Deltoid muscle	See above.

Extension of the upper arm (movement towards the rear)

Deltoid muscle	See above.
Latissimus dorsi muscle	See above.
Trapezius muscle	See above.
Rhomboid muscles	See above.

The rotator muscles

The acromion forms the bony ceiling of the shoulder joint. The humeral head is covered and stabilised by the powerful tendons of the rotator muscles. These muscles, in conjunction with the coraco-humeral ligament and the powerfully developed shoulder joint muscles, hold the head of the humerus in the socket. The head of the humerus is held against the acromion by the uppermost sections of the rotator muscles, formed by the tendon of the supraspinatus muscle. The same tendon prevents the head of the humerus being drawn up against the acromion and blocked when abduction of the arm through the deltoid muscle commences. The points of attachment of the rotator muscles are in the vicinity of the rotation axis (6).

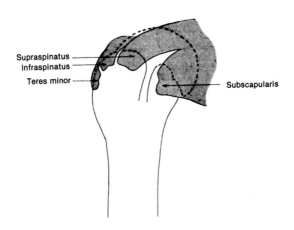

6 The rotator muscles, seen from the front.
After: R. Cailliet: Shoulder Pain, F.A. Davis Company, 1967.

The tendons of the following muscles together form the rotator muscles:

Abduction

Supraspinatus muscle	See above.

External rotation

Infraspinatus muscle	Extends from the infraspinous fossa and the lateral edge of the shoulder blade to the greater tuberosity of the humerus.
Innervation:	Suprascapular nerve (C5–C6).
Teres minor muscle	Extends from the axillary edge of the shoulder blade to the greater tuberosity of the humerus.
Innervation:	Circumflex nerve (C4–C5).

Internal rotation

Subscapularis muscle	Extends from the subscapular fossa to the lesser tuberosity of the humerus.
Teres major muscle	Extends from the lower angle of the shoulder blade to the crest of the lesser tuberosity of the humerus.

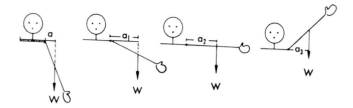

7 **The weight of the arm** causes maximum torsion when the arm is abducted relative to the shoulder blade by 90°. The lever arm (a) on which the weight (W) acts is determined by the distance to the vertical line through the centre of gravity of the arm and the rotational axis of the joint.
After: Williams and Lissner: Biomechanics of Human Motion. W.B. Saunders Co., 1962.

Both subscapularis and teres major are innervated by the subscapular nerve (C5–C6).

Functional mobility
A fully functional shoulder joint should make it possible to raise the hand to the nape of the neck and on to the back, so that we can dress and undress ourselves, comb our hair and perform our bodily and toilet hygiene without any need of assistance from others. In most people, the arm can be abducted up to about 90°, while flexion is also possible to approximately 90°, and internal and external rotation both amount to about 60°, enabling us to perform all these daily tasks.

The weight of the upper extremities accounts for approximately 5% of total body weight. The centre of gravity of the arm is normally situated at approximately the height of the upper arm epicondyle. The torsion created by the weight of the arm rises on abduction and flexion of the upper arm, reaches its maximum at approximately 90° (**7**) and then falls again. Stressing of the shoulder joint therefore increases during activities involving the upper arm in the abducted or flexed position, particularly if the arm is additionally stressed while in these positions (Inmann et al. 1944, Williams and Lissner 1962).

The joints of the shoulder girdle in inflammatory diseases of the joints
In chronic polyarthritis, the joints of the shoulder girdle are affected in approximately 60% of patients, in ankylosing spondylitis, the figure is about 30%. In most cases, the disorder is primarily a synovitis of the humeroscapular or acromioclavicular joint, with swelling of the capsule and effusion. Minor effusions in the humeroscapular joint can scarcely be diagnosed by clinical means, whereas major effusions

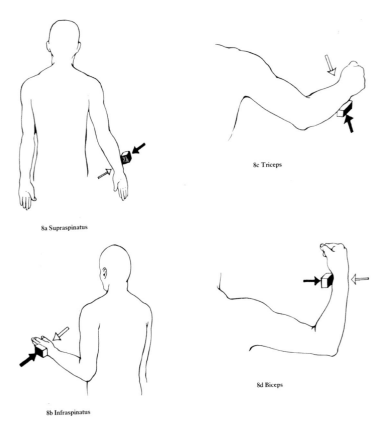

8a Supraspinatus

8c Triceps

8b Infraspinatus

8d Biceps

8 a–d: Examination of the muscle attachments.
After: J.G.Chusid and J.J.McDonald: Correlative Neuroanatomy & Functional Neurology, Lange Medical Publications, 1967.

cause the joint to swell up like a balloon under the deltoid muscle. Inflammation can, however, also be observed in the joint between the clavicle and the sternum (sternoclavicular joint). Synovitis leads to increased friction between cartilage surfaces, as the lubricating ability of the inflamed joint fluid is reduced. The force required for movement in the inflamed joint increases considerably. However, since the force applied is greatly reduced by the pain, patients normally scarcely move their shoulders, which leads to shrinkage of the capsule and the adjacent muscles.

Inflammation of the tendons and tenosynovitides can often occur in the region of the shoulders, around the rotator muscles and the long biceps muscles. This type of damage to the tendons reduces the stabilising effect of the rotator muscles and the long biceps tendon. If the rotator muscles become thin in the region of the supraspinatus tendon, and if perforation of the rotator muscles and the development of a hole occurs, then the head of the humerus will be pulled upwards against the acromion by the contraction of the deltoid muscle, so that the mechanical conditions for movement in the shoulder joint rapidly deteriorate. In time, the functional ability of the shoulder joint will be considerably impaired not only by the pain, but also by the destruction and fibrous reduction in size of the muscular apparatus and tendons, as well as the joint capsules, and by the fibrous changes in the synovial membrane and the erosion of cartilage. Inflammation of the tendons and tendon sheaths can usually be diagnosed by palpation and by applying stress to the muscle and tendon attachment points (8) (Pettersson 1984).

The elbow joint

Anatomy and function

The elbow joint acts like a hinge and permits bending and stretching of the forearm. In conjunction with the proximal and distal radio-ulnar joints, it also enables the forearm to be rotated around its axis. These movements are known as pronation and supination, depending on which way the hand faces.

Movements of the elbow joint

Bending (flexion)

Biceps brachii muscle	See under shoulder joint.
Brachialis muscle	Extends from the front side of the humerus to the coronoid process of the ulna.
Innervation:	Musculocutaneus nerve (C5–C6).
Brachioradialis muscle, extensor carpi radialis longus and extensor carpi radialis brevis muscles	Extend from the radial epicondyle of the humerus to the hand, i.e. the styloid process of the radius and the metacarpals II and III.
Innervation:	Radial nerve (C6–C7–C8).

Flexor carpi radialis muscle Palmaris longus muscle	Extend from the ulnar epicondyle of the humerus to the hand and attach to metacarpals II, III and V and to the palmar aponeurosis.
Innervation:	Median nerve (C6–C7).
Flexor carpi ulnaris muscle	Also extends from the ulnar epicondyle of the humerus to the hand and attaches to the pisiform bone and to metacarpal V.
Innervation:	Ulnar nerve (C8–T1).

Stretching (extension)

Triceps brachii muscle	See under shoulder joint.
Anconeus muscle	Extends from the radial epicondyle of the humerus to the olecranon.
Innervation:	Radial nerve (C5–C7).

Supination

Biceps brachii muscle	See under shoulder joint.
Supinator muscle	Extends from the radial epicondyle of the humerus to the radius.
Innervation:	Radial nerve (C5–C7).

Pronation

Pronator teres muscle	Extends from the ulnar epicondyle of the humerus and from the coronoid process of the ulna to the volar radial surface.
Pronator quadratus muscle	Extends from the volar side of the ulna to the radius
Innervation:	Median nerve (C7–T1).

Functional mobility
Applying weight to the forearm when in a flexed position can lead to enormous stress in the elbow, as both the powerful flexor and extensor muscles of this joint have to act over a short lever arm (**9**).

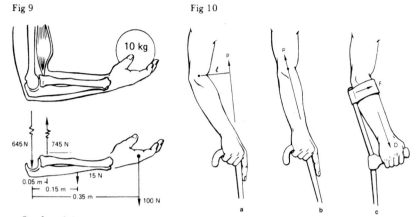

Fig 9   Fig 10

645 N   745 N

0.05 m

0.15 m

0.35 m

15 N

100 N

10 kg

9   **A weight of 10 kg can create compression of up to 65 kg in the elbow** (Williams and Lissner 1962).

10   a) **Stressing the elbow as a result of using a stick or an elbow crutch.** P = weight transferred to the stick. P × l = torsion resulting from the load. **b)** If the elbow joint is extended when applying the weight to the stick, the torsion is reduced – and with it the necessary tensioning of the extensor muscles – as a result of shortening of the effective lever arm, which ideally would be reduced to zero. **c)** Forearm crutch with the wrist in functional position.
After: Williams and Lissner: Biomechanics of Human Motion. W.B.Saunders & Co., 1962.

The torsion in these muscles changes with the angle of the elbow and reaches its maximum at 90° (Williams and Lissner 1962). Stressing the triceps muscle in the elbow, for example, by using a walking stick, can lead to considerable intra-articular increases in pressure when the arm is bent. The force which causes this compression is the sum of the weight resting on the stick and the contraction force of the triceps muscle. The length of the lever arm naturally plays an important role (**10**). These relationships must be taken into careful consideration when it comes to determining the optimal length of stick.

Pronation and supination are very important in daily life, for instance in turning taps on and off, turning a key in the lock, opening a wine bottle with a corkscrew. Here again, considerable intra-articular forces have to be reckoned with.

The elbow joint in chronic polyarthritis
In ca. 60% of all cases, chronic polyarthritis leads to synovitis of the elbow joint and this can cause pain both on movement and when resting. Very often, pronation and supination are painful and restricted and can pose a threat to functional capacity similar to that represented by flexion and extension contracture. The condition can

take the form of inflammation of the humero-ulnar or humeroradial joints, and the proximal and even distal radio-ulnar joints. In ankylosing spondylitis, on the other hand, the elbow is only rarely affected, though in juvenile chronic polyarthritis it is frequently involved in the process.

It is by no means rare for the ulnar nerve to be affected in the region of the elbow joint, especially in its sulcus, by proliferation of synovial or capsule tissue. The nerve can be damaged by compression or inflammatory infiltration, in which case the sensory capacity on the ulnar side of the hand, and especially the function of the small muscles of the hand and the flexor carpi ulnaris are impaired. Not infrequently, the ulnar nerve has grown together with the inflamed or already scarred joint capsule. In such cases, mobilisation of the elbow joint under anaesthetic or corrective measures for a flexion or extension contracture using plastic casts can cause severe and generally irreparable damage to the nerve. Any corrective manipulation of the elbow joint should therefore be attempted only with the greatest care. As a rule, it is advisable to make a preliminary revision and possibly move the nerve to the flexor (anterior) surface of the elbow.

Inflammation of the tendons of the elbow muscles can also give rise to pain and these conditions are also best diagnosed by palpation and applying pressure to the attachment points.

The wrist

Anatomy and function
The wrist comprises the joint between the radius and the carpus, the joints between the various wrist bones and the joints between the latter and the metacarpal bones. The radiocarpal joint is formed by the concave surface of the radius and the convex surfaces of the scaphoid, the lunate bone and the triquetral bone. This joint is separated from the distal radio-ulnar joint by means of an articular disc, so that the ulna does not in fact form any part of the wrist. The distal row of wrist bones is made up of the trapezium and trapezoid bone, the capitate bone and the hamate bone, all of which are connected by joints with the metacarpal bones. Bending and stretching of the wrist, as well as ulnar and radial flexion, mainly take place in the radiocarpal joint. This part of the joint is in the form of an 'egg joint' and allows relatively large and finely differentiated movement.

The muscles of the hand
The extensor tendons of the hand and the fingers run in their tendon sheaths under the transverse stabilising ligaments on the back of the

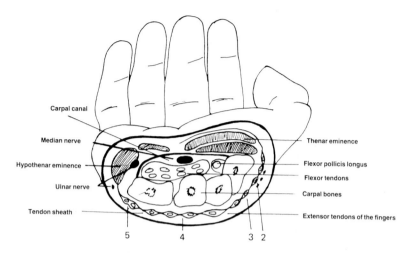

11 **Section through the hand** on a level with the carpal canal.

hand. The tendon sheaths are divided up into six dorsal tendon fans, composed of the tendons of the following muscles:

1 Abductor pollicis longus and extensor pollicis brevis.
2 Extensor carpi radialis brevis and longus.
3 Extensor pollicis longus.
4 Extensor digitorum communis and extensor indicis proprius.
5 Extensor digiti minimi.
6 Extensor carpi ulnaris.

On the volar side of the wrist are the tendons of the flexor digitorum sublimis muscle and the flexor digitorum profundus muscle, which run in a common sheath through the carpal canal, under the powerful transverse ligament of the carpus volar. Arranged radially to this bundle of tendons are the median nerve and the tendon of the flexor pollicis longus muscle, whereas on the ulnar side of the carpal canal, the ulnar nerve on its own extends through the fibrous loge de Guyon and over the wrist (**11**).

Function of the wrist
For normal hand functions such as are required for most tasks in daily life, but also for sport, or in playing the piano or the violin etc., a functional position allowing a range of ca. 20° extension, 25–40° flexion and a certain circumduction is called for. In a very large number of activities, supination is absolutely essential as well.

Examples are grasping cylindrical objects, turning keys, giving and taking money, writing and many types of manual work. Restricted supination can be caused by diseases of both the proximal and distal radio-ulnar joints.

The wrist in inflammatory diseases of the joints

In classic chronic polyarthritis, one usually finds synovitides in the region of the wrist and the tendon sheaths (Brewerton 1957, Brewerton and Lettin 1974, Millender *et al.* 1975). Synovitis leads to pain on movement and to a restriction of movement in all directions. After a certain time, X-rays will show a loss of substance in the distal sections of the forearm bones. Erosion of the styloid process of the ulna and subchondral cysts in the radius are characteristic of this condition, the latter being compared by Mannerfelt to crypts. The wrist bones occasionally slide in the direction of the ulna, so that a diastasis can occur between the scaphoid and lunate bone. The reason for the frequent instability of the wrist is to be found in the destruction of the ligament apparatus. The result of such an ulnar shift in the proximal wrist bones is a slight radial deviation in the metacarpal bones. This deformity is generally regarded as one of the causes of ulnar drift in the fingers. The resulting zigzag deformity is also known as 'scoliosis of the hand' (Pahle and Raunio 1969, Shapiro *et al.* 1968/**12**).

In chronic polyarthritis, a gradual breakdown of the cartilage and the bone underneath it occurs very frequently, the ligaments being

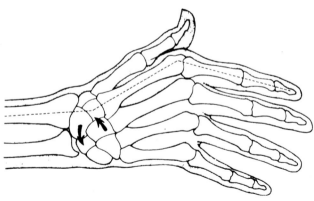

12   Typical deformity in the rheumatic hand: Zigzag phenomenon or scoliosis of the hand with radial deviation of the metacarpal bones and ulnar deviation of the long fingers.
After: J.L.Melvin: Rheumatic Disease: Occupational Therapy and Rehabilitation. F.A.Davis Co., 1977.

stretched and destroyed and stability reduced. Not infrequently, volar subluxation or even luxation of the wrist occurs too.

Tenosynovitides of the extensor tendons on the back of the hand are extremely frequent and generally appear at the onset of the disease. The formation and growth of rheumatic granulation tissue leads to a weakening and to rupture of the extensor tendons. The sharp edges which frequently develop on the dorsal side of the caput ulnae in the course of the rheumatic process can fray the extensor tendons of the fifth finger to start with, then those of the fourth, then the third, and sometimes even those of the second finger, finally leading to rupture (Bäckdahl 1963). Similar mechanical wear is also possible on the edges of the bones in the volar region (Vaughan-Jackson 1958, Mannerfelt and Norman 1969, Mannerfelt 1984). One can also mention here that the long extensor tendon of the thumb can rupture as a result of severe tenosynovitis, quite independently of other symptoms and signs.

The tendons of the extensor carpi radialis longus and brevis and of the extensor carpi ulnaris are attached to the dorsal surface of the radial and ulnar side of the second, third and fifth metacarpal bones, while the tendons of the flexor carpi radialis and of the flexor carpi ulnaris are attached to the volar side of the second and third metacarpals and the pisiform or hamate bone. Tenosynovitides in this area are often painful and can also be the cause of deformities developing. This can easily be demonstrated by specially loading the tendons in a similar manner to that described earlier with regard to the shoulder joint.

Inflammation of the tendon sheaths in the carpal canal can affect the mobility of the fingers. Trapping of the median nerve can lead to the carpal tunnel syndrome, with a loss of sensitivity in the region of the thumb, the index finger and middle finger. More rarely, the ulnar nerve can become compressed in the loge de Guyon.

The hand

Anatomy and function

The hand serves as a gripping instrument capable of developing considerable force but also displaying the highest precision (Cailliet 1975). From an anatomical point of view the radial part of the hand with its highly differentiated system of joints for the thumb and index finger is designed for precision motor functions and endowed with great mobility, whereas the remaining three fingers on the ulnar side

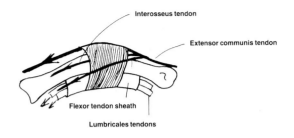

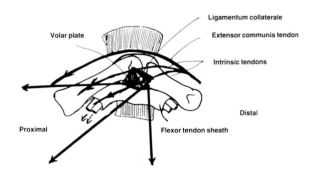

13   Schematic representation of the metacarpophalangeal joints.

are more suitable for gripping cylindrical objects, or for support or for catching, and can develop considerable force.

Anatomically, the hand can be seen as a unit made up of two transverse arches and a third arch running in a longitudinal direction (Flatt 1968). The proximal transverse arch is made up of the eight small wrist bones. The distal transverse arch is made up of the metacarpophalangeal joints, which are generally slightly flexed. The stability of the whole is ensured by a differentiated system of ligaments (Hagert 1978).

The metacarpophalangeal joints (MCP) (13)
The proximal joints of the fingers are shaped in such a way that the fingers can generally be moved in any direction from the neutral position (0°) or a slightly flexed position. In a position of 90° flexion, however, they are normally sufficiently stable to be able to withstand attempts to incline them to the side. On the dorsal side, the surfaces of the joints are broader, and on the volar side somewhat narrower. Lateral stability is provided by the collateral ligaments, which are under maximum tension when in the flexed position, and extremely slack in the extended position. Looked at schematically, they consist

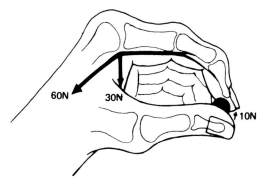

14 The finger-tip hold. If one reaches for a small object, then the flexor tendons, shown here in black, are flexed. If a pressure of 10 N is exerted between thumb and index finger, then there is a tensile load of 60 N exerted axially on the forearm and one of approximately 30 N exerted tangentially in the direction of the palm.

of two parts, one distal which is attached to the base of the bottom phalanges, and a proximal part which is attached to the volar cartilage plate. In addition, the small muscles of the hand act on the MCP joints, in particular the interaction of the interossei muscles to produce a stablising effect. On the flexor aspect, the tendons of the flexor digitorum sublimis and the flexor digitorum profundus run in their sheaths, held in each finger by the annular ligaments. Fibrous structures which contain cartilage – the so-called volar plate – which reinforces them, strengthen the capsule apparatus on the volar side and also the stability of the MCP joints. The tendons of the flexor digitorum sublimis are attached to the base of the middle phalanges, while those of the profundus are attached to the base of the distal phalanges. The corresponding muscles flex the proximal or the distal interphalangeal joints (PIP or DIP joints).

If one attempts to flex the MCP joints against resistance, there is a marked increase in intra-articular pressure. The tangential forces force the annular ligament, the volar plate and the bottom phalanges into the hand (Smith *et al.* 1964). In order to achieve a 'pincer force' of 10 N, a flexing force of 60 N must be exercised in the MCP joint, while there would be a force of 30 N to be taken up on the volar side. These values are based on isolated tests carried out on the long hand muscles. Recent tests indicate that under normal circumstances, the pressures are considerably higher (Chao *et al.* 1976/**14**).

The muscles of the hand
The enormous variety of functional possibilities of the hand is based on the interaction of the long muscles from the forearm (extrinsic

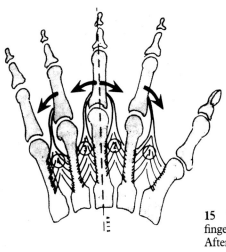

15 **The dorsal interossei** abduct the fingers.
After R. Cailliet: Hand Pain and Impairment, F.A. Davis Co., 1975.

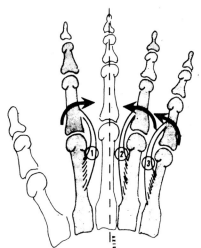

16 **The volar interossei** adduct the fingers, bending the bottom joint and stretching the middle joint.

muscles) with the small muscles of the hand (intrinsic muscles). By the latter, we mean those muscles which have their origin on the other side of the wrist and their insertion at the metacarpal bones or phalanges. The functional movements of the hands are always the result of a precisely coordinated interaction of agonists and their synergists in the intrinsic and extrinsic muscles. The long flexors flex the PIP and DIP joints, while the volar interossei and the lumbricales flex the MCP joints and extend the PIP joints through their attachment points on the long extensor tendons in the region of the middle phalanges. Normally, they also have an extending effect on the top phalanges through their attachment to the extensor communis tendon. The tendons of the extensor digitorum communis act on all three joints of the individual long fingers. Adduction of the fingers is effected by the three volar interossei muscles, while abduction is the responsibility of the four dorsal interossei muscles (**15** and **16**).

Innervation of the hand muscles
Historically, the ulnar nerve (C8–T1) is the oldest nerve in the hand and innervates the entire intrinsic muscular apparatus with the exception of the two radial lumbricales, the abductor pollicis brevis and approximately half of the flexor pollicis brevis and opponens pollicis, which are served by the median nerve (C6–C7). The deep end of the flexor pollicis brevis is innervated by the ulnar nerve. The radial nerve (C5–C6) serves the short and long extensor pollicis and the abductor pollicis longus. The thumb is thus controlled by all three hand nerves in concert.

Functional mobility of the hand
Various classifications have been put forward to describe the different grasps possible with the hand (Napier 1956).

Cylindrical grasp

With the cylindrical grasp, all the fingers are bent around the object to be held, while the opposing thumb closes the grip. The long flexor tendons in particular are activated for this grasp. The muscle elements pulling on the three ulnar fingers are particularly powerful.

Finger-tip grasp

This grasp, to which we have already referred, is carried out with the tips of the thumb and index finger. A variant of this is the so-called key grip, where an object is grasped between the thumb and the radial side of the index finger, as is the case when a key is turned in the lock. Quite frequently, the middle finger is used for support; more rarely the ring finger too. A healthy hand is capable of innumerable variations on this grasp, due to the high degree of differentiation which the sensory and motor equipment of the hand is capable of, as well as the high level of mobility of all the joints involved.

The ball grasp

The third type of grasp is the ball grasp, in which considerable importance is attached to the high level of mobility of the thumb and its opposition, with the hypothenar eminence, to the little finger. When kneading and in similar activities, this grasp is subjected to a constant change from precision to force and back again, with a sophisticated interaction between the intrinsic and extrinsic muscles.

In recent years, new ways have been developed to give a quantitative description of the grasping functions of the hand (Sollermann and Sperling 1977, Sperling 1979). These are used above all to assist comparison between the functions of the hand before and after surgical intervention.

The healthy hand already has a tendency towards ulnar deviation on the part of the long fingers, because of the increased mobility of the ulnar components in the volar direction. A very firm grasp thus brings about a slight ulnar deviation of the fingers. The flexor tendons also form an angle open in the direction of the ulna as they pass through the ligamenta annularia, in the normal course of events. The component of force acting in the direction of the ulna is proportional to the strength of the grasp. For the function of the healthy hand, this does not seem important.

The hand in inflammatory diseases of the joints

Chronic arthritis of the MCP joints accompanied by exudation can very rapidly lead to stretching of the capsules and the volar plate and thus to instability because the mechanical stress imposed by the long flexor tendons is very considerable (Brewerton 1974, Flatt 1968, Millender and Nalebuff 1975b, Swezey 1971, Smith et al. 1964, 1966). This instability is at the same time the starting point and the precondition for the development of subluxations. This type of deformity on the part of the MCP joints is initially only visible under stress, but in advanced stages, it is also obvious in the rest position (**13**).

Ulnar deviation

Ulnar deviation of the fingers has many and varied causes. The most important of these are:

- the natural tendency of the hand towards ulnar deviation, due to its structures
- imbalance between the two collateral ligaments of each individual bottom joint, the radial being the weaker
- imbalance between radial and ulnar muscles

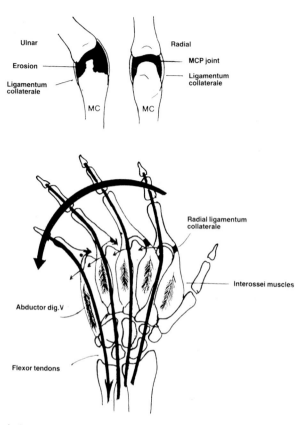

17 Ulnar deviation.

- synovitis and capsulitis in the MCP joint, loosening of the weak fibrous fixation apparatus of the long extensor tendons and sliding down from the back of the metacarpal capitulum in the direction of the ulna, into the sulcus between the metacarpal capitula

- rotation of the carpal bones and the radial deviation of the metacarpal bones

The contraction of the long flexor tendons of the fourth and fifth fingers also contains an element of movement directed towards the ulna (**17**).

A basic precondition of the development of any deformity is the instability of the joints, but any external stress, e.g. any stress brought about by movements performed in the course of one's daily life, will

51

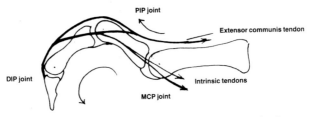

Normal: active flexing of the middle and top joints with passive overextension of the bottom joint

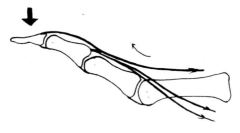

Intrinsic contracture: attempt at flexing in the middle and end joints, with passive hyperextension of the bottom joints

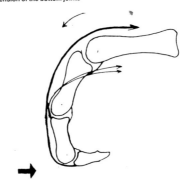

Attempt at active flexing of middle and top joints, with passively flexed bottom joint

18   Intrinsic contracture.

contribute to it, as will any stress imposed internally by the tendons. Fearnley (1952) has described three stages of ulnar deviation, using clinical criteria: Grade I: actively reducible. Grade II: passively reducible. Grade III: fixed, not reducible.

Swan neck deformity
Swan neck deformity can occur with disorders of the flexing mechanism of the hand, for example, extensive tenosynovitides in the flexor tendons. These are normally accompanied by synovitides in

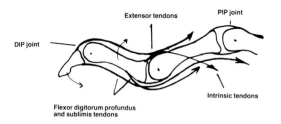

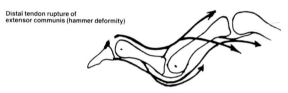

19 Swan neck deformity.

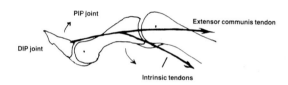

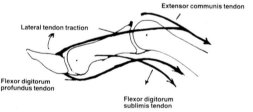

20 Buttonhole deformity.

the MCP and PIP joints. Contractures in the region of the intrinsic muscles (**18**) often occur as a reflex. The hammer finger deformity occurs where the extensor tendons tear away from their points of attachment at the bottom of the top phalanges of the fingers. The complete swan neck deformity consists of a fixed overextension in the middle joint and a flexed position in the end joint, which can no longer be extended actively.

Initially, this deformity can be actively corrected (Grade I) or is at least passively reducible (Grade II). If the principal cause of the

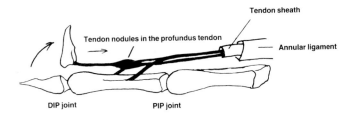

Tendon sheath

Tendon nodules in the profundus tendon

Annular ligament

DIP joint

PIP joint

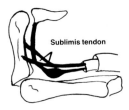

With the PIP joint extended, the DIP joint can be flexed

Sublimis tendon

With the PIP and DIP joints flexed, the tendon nodule in the profundus tendon is very close to the entrance to the sublimis tendon. If the nodule increases in size, it will no longer be able to pass through the entrance into the sublimis tendon, and the finger can no longer be extended or will jerk.

21 Tendon nodules in the flexor tendon canal.

deformity, such as nodules in the flexor tendons and/or synovitis of the middle joints cannot be successfully treated, then the PIP joints will stiffen in a position of the hyperextension (Grade III). If the subcutaneous soft parts and the skin on the dorsal side of the finger should contract as well, then the finger would become functionally useless (Millender and Nalebuff 1975/**19**).

Buttonhole deformity
The so-called buttonhole deformity can develop as a result of destruction of the extensor aponeurosis on the dorsal side of the PIP joints caused by inflammation spreading from the joint to the tendons. Synovitides and exudation, together with stretching of the capsule, can lead to the extensor tendons slipping down to the side, or to rupturing, with both sides slipping down. Traction in the extensor apparatus no longer leads to extension of the middle joint, but to flexion. In this way, the middle joints lose their capacity for active extension (**20**).

The same change can occur if the extension is hindered by tendon nodules in the flexor tendon canal. In Sweden, we say that the button will no longer go through the buttonhole (**21**).

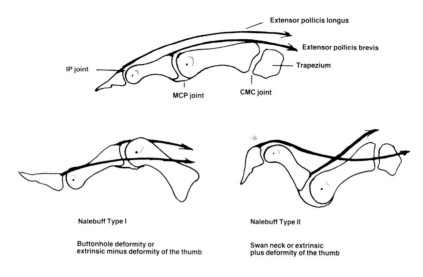

Extensor pollicis longus

Extensor pollicis brevis

Trapezium

IP joint

MCP joint

CMC joint

Nalebuff Type I

Buttonhole deformity or
extrinsic minus deformity of the thumb

Nalebuff Type II

Swan neck or extrinsic
plus deformity of the thumb

22   Thumb deformities.

Typical deformities of the thumbs
Deformities of the thumbs frequently occur in chronic polyarthritis
(Nalebuff 1969, 1984/22).

Synovitides in the MCP joint of the thumb lead to enlargement of
the capsule, to subluxation of the base of the bottom phalanx in a volar
direction and in time, to a change in the direction in which the
extensor tendons run. The extensor pollicis brevis muscle loses
contact with the bottom phalanx. The result is flexion contracture in
the MCP joint and overextension in the IP joint (Nalebuff Type I,
buttonhole or extrinsic minus thumb deformity). So long as no
overextension contracture occurs in the IP joint, and stability remains
more or less assured, this deformity does not yet represent a serious
impairment of function. With arthritis in the proximal joint of the
thumb, flexion or adduction contracture in the CMC joint may occur
as a reaction to the inflammatory process. The patient tries to
compensate for the deformity by overextension of the MCP joint, as a
result of which the long extensor tendon of the thumb becomes too
long and the IP can no longer be actively extended (Nalebuff Type II,
swan neck or extrinsic plus thumb deformity). Thumb deformities
can, however, also occur as a result of tendon rupture. Pathologically

damaged thumb joints can in time become the cause of many functional disorders and require surgical intervention. Frequently, arthrodesis in the MCP joint and/or in the IP joint is indicated, to restore the ability to use a finger-tip grip.

The carpal tunnel syndrome
Tendon sheath inflammation on the flexor side can lead to pressure damage to the median nerve as a result of compression in the carpal tunnel, causing the carpal tunnel syndrome. With this condition, the patient frequently experiences paraesthesia and pain in the night, radiating out to the thumb, index and middle fingers, as well as hypoaesthesia in the skin in the area of distribution of the median nerve. In advanced cases, it can result in thenar atrophy.

In the region of the palm and the volar sides of the fingers, tendon inflammation often takes the form of nodules which can lead to disturbance of the finger functions. It can lead to flexion contracture or, more commonly, the finger will jerk. The nodules are particularly unpleasant if the tendon sheaths or the hole formed by the annular ligament is constricted by rheumatic inflammation or secondary scarring processes (tenovaginitis stenosans). Ruptures of the flexor tendons, mostly starting with the long flexor tendon of the thumb when passing bony spurs, are not uncommon (Mannerfelt 1969, Nalebuff 1975, Souter 1979, Helal 1984).

Dorsal tenosynovitis in the wrist, caput ulnae syndrome
Inflammation of the dorsal tendon sheaths can lead to pressure on the blood vessels, as a result of tissue proliferation, leading to a reduction of the blood supply. In this way too, the tendons in the sheaths can be destroyed. Another mechanism is the fraying of the extensor tendons caused by sharp edges on the caput ulnae, due to erosion. A third mechanism leads to tendon rupture as a result of the formation of rheumatic tissue within the tendons, or of such tissue growing into the tendons from the outside.

The back

Anatomy and function
As a rule, the spine consists of 7 cervical vertebrae, 12 thoracic vertebrae, and 5 lumbar vertebrae. The bodies of the vertebrae are connected with one another by intervertebral discs. These are primary fibrocartilaginous joints, rather than joints in the normal sense. The bodies of the vertebrae are also connected and stabilised by

a powerful apparatus of longitudinal ligaments which completely enclose them and which also provide part of the front wall of the vertebral canal. As already mentioned, only the so-called head joints – between occiput, atlas and axis – are joints in the true sense and constructed without benefit of discs. The intervertebral discs are of hard connective tissue containing a great deal of fibrous matter, with hyaline cartilage containing much fibrous matter facing the bony upper plates of the bodies of the vertebrae, and a softer but inelastic gelatinous nucleus. Because of their construction, they have especially good 'shock absorber' characteristics.

Each vertebra has at the back two pairs of articular processes – one upper and one lower pair – with joint surfaces for the small vertebral joints, by way of which further contacts are made to the vertebrae above or below them. These small vertebral joints are joints in the strict sense, i.e. their joint surfaces are covered with hyaline cartilage and their joint capsules are lined with a synovial membrane. All these joints have a fibrous rudimentary intervertebral disc, whose shape reminds one of the menisci in the knee joints.

The alignment of the joint surfaces of the small vertebral joints determines the axes or directions, around or in which the appropriate segment of the spine can be moved. The small vertebral joints at the back of the cervical spine are aligned in a dorsoventral direction in such a way that they rise moderately from back to front, thus permitting the movement in the sagittal plane already described. The capsule and ligament apparatus is, however, sufficiently broad to ensure the degree of rotation and lateral flexion already mentioned.

The cartilaginous joint surfaces of the small vertebral joints of the thoracic spine are oriented towards the front. The joint surfaces of the upper processes of the thoracic vertebrae point more to the front than to the side, while the cartilaginous joint surfaces of the lower processes are aligned correspondingly more in a ventral direction, and a little towards the medial. The arrangement described and the corresponding capsule and ligament apparatus allows a moderate amount of movement in the sagittal plane and the frontal plane, but a relatively good amount of movement for rotation. Each thoracic vertebra is also connected by way of two genuine joints with its pair of ribs. The stability of the thoracic spine is strengthened by the thoracic cage. Nevertheless, this stability is not sufficient to prevent severe deformities occurring in the case of paralysis, after fractures or destructive disease processes in the region of the thoracic vertebrae.

In the upper and middle section of the lumbar spine, the cartilaginous and bony surface joints of the small vertebral joints are aligned in a sagittal or almost sagittal direction. Their joint cavity is thus clearly visible in X-rays taken in a sagittal direction. The preferred movement is in the sagittal plane, and the relatively broad capsules also permit a good measure of lateral flexion, while the rotation in the region of the lumbar spine is relatively small.

Between each pair of vertebrae, the intervertebral foramina, through which the nerve roots and blood vessels emerge from the spinal canal, are kept free by the surrounding bone and tissue structures. Because of the different rates of growth of the spinal cord and the spinal column, the height of a segment of spinal cord does not correspond to the height of the associated vertebra. At the level of the 6th cervical vertebra, the difference is about the height of the body of a vertebra, by the middle of the thoracic spine it is about twice that amount, and the spinal cord ends on a level with the first lumbar vertebra. The lumbar, sacral and coccygeal nerve roots form the so-called cauda equina. The intervertebral discs are normally compressible and thus permit the spinal column a relatively large amount of freedom of all-round movement. At maximum flexion, the distance between the spines of the 7th cervical vertebra and the 1st sacral vertebra in a healthy individual of middle age increases by about 15 cm, as compared with maximum extension. Finally, the vertebral arches are connected with one another by short ligaments, the so-called ligamenta flava, and their spines by a longitudinal apparatus of ligaments.

The upright posture is made possible by the fine coordination of the proprioceptive nerves in the joints, ligaments and muscles. One is tempted to make a comparison with the rigging of a tall-masted sailing ship, for as long as the mast is in equilibrium, the rigging is not under any particular strain. However, if the mast inclines slightly, the rigging on the other side is put under tension in order to stabilise the mast. In the case of the spinal column, the place of the rigging is taken by the muscles. Muscles of different lengths act in different ways on the various segments of the spine. It is therefore possible to concentrate the contraction force on that part of the spinal column which requires special stabilisation (Brunnström 1966). The upright posture of man has led to the cervical and lumbar spine forming an arch (lordosis) which is open to the rear, while the thoracic spine forms an arch that is open to the front (kyphosis). The centre of gravity of the body, when the individual is standing in a normal posture in an intermediate position lies in front of the 11th thoracic vertebra. Further details on the anatomy of the spinal column and the entire back can be found in the appropriate textbooks.

58

The spinal column in inflammatory diseases of the joints

Osteopenia (reduced bone mass) normally develops in women after the menopause. This differs from the development of the bones in ageing men, in whom it is rare to find osteopenia in excess of what one would expect from atrophy resulting from inactivity. More severe forms of osteopenia can have different causes, among them the sort of immobilisation necessitated by rheumatic diseases or the use of certain medicaments such as corticosteroids.

Ankylosing spondylitis mostly starts with backache as a result of inflammation of the sacro-iliac joints. The disease then spreads via the small vertebral joints and the intervertebral disc connections of the entire spinal column, and also takes in the joints between vertebrae and ribs. The thoracic kyphosis becomes more pronounced as a result of progressive fibrosis and ossification of the long ligaments of the spinal column, while the lumbar spine is extended and frequently compensates by increasing the lordosis of the cervical spine. This leads to the type of posture, often found with the disease, in which the head is pushed forward. However, if there is no cervical lordosis, then the head flexion deformity fortunately rarely seen nowadays can develop. An early warning of the disease on X-rays is the osteopenia of the bodies of the vertebrae (shiny corners), which in side projection take the form of inclined rectangles. In the final stages, an X-ray of the spinal column taken from the front, with its ossified ligaments, would look like a stick of bamboo.

From a functional point of view, the stiffening of the spinal column in kyphosis means a restriction of the patient's field of vision. As the kyphosis increases, and with insufficient lordosis in the neck, the patient is forced to direct his eyes straight downwards, for which he can only compensate by bending the hip and knee joints. Flexion contracture of the hip and knee joints may develop. Inflammatory changes and the bony ankylosis of the costovertebral joints finally lead to a stiffening of the thoracic cage and impair breathing (Moll 1980).

Lower extremities

The hip joint

Anatomy and function

The hip joint is a stable ball-and-socket joint which is deeply embedded in the fossa acetabuli and protected by a strong joint capsule, powerful ligaments and strong muscles. In spite of the high degree of stability, the mobility of the joint is considerable, even greater than is required for the normal functions performed during our daily lives.

The muscles of the hip joint

Hip flexors

Iliopsoas muscle	Extends from the iliac fossa and the vertebrae T12–L5 to the lesser trochanter of the femur.
Innervation:	Femoral nerve (L2–L4).
Rectus femoris muscle	Extends from the anterior inferior iliac spine and the acetabulum to the tubercle of the tibia. The four heads together form the strong, broad quadriceps tendon, in which the knee cap as the largest sesamoid bone in the human body is embedded.
Innervation:	Femoral nerve (L2–L4).
Tensor fasciae latae muscle	Extends from the iliac crest to the iliotibial tract.
Innervation:	Superior gluteal nerve (L4–L5).

The muscles of the rectus femoris strengthen the front part of the hip joint capsule, take up the vastus medialis and vastus lateralis and, together with these, form the quadriceps muscle with the ligamentum patellae attached to the tubercle of the tibia. In this way, the complex of muscles extends over two joints, acting as flexors in the hip joint and as extensors in the knee joint.

Hip extensors

Gluteus maximus muscle	Has its origin at the iliac crest, the fascia lumbodorsalis and the sacrum and attaches to the tuberositas glutea femoris, but also connects with the iliotibial tract in part.
Innervation:	Inferior gluteal nerve (L5–S2).
Semitendinosus and semi-membranosus muscles	Extend from the ischial tuberosity of the pelvis to the pes anserinus on the medial side of the proximal tibia.

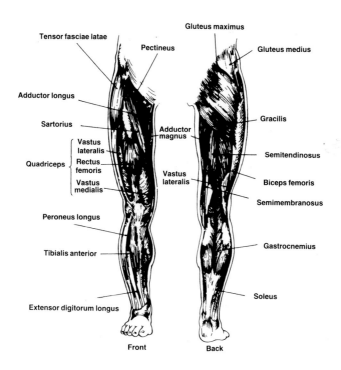

23   The muscles of the leg.

Innervation:	Medial popliteal nerve (L4–S1).
Biceps femoris muscle	Has its origin at the ischial tuberosity of the pelvis and extends both to the head of the fibula and also to the rear side of the head of the tibia.
Innervation:	Sciatic nerve (L4–S1).

A part of the adductor magnus muscle, which extends from the pubic bone to the femur, also acts as an extensor for the hip.

Hip abductors

The most important abductor is the

Gluteus medius muscle	Extends from the iliac crest and ileum to the greater trochanter.
Innervation:	Superior gluteal nerve (L4–L5).

From a slightly flexed position, the tensor fasciae latae with the powerful tendon fibres of the lateral sections of the gluteus maximus attaching to it, acts as a powerful hip abductor muscle and hip stabiliser.

Hip adductors

Adductor magnus and adductor longus muscles	Extend from the pubic bone to the medial surface of the femur.
Innervation:	Obturator nerve (L2–L4).

The other medial muscles of the thigh, such as the semimembranosus and semitendinosus but also the sartorius, act synergistically to assist with adduction of the thigh.

All those muscles which act on two joints, such as the biceps, the semimembranosus, the semitendinosus, the quadriceps, the tensor fasciae latae, the gracilis and the sartorius, are heavily dependent for their effect on the position of the other joint. For example, the biceps femoris and the semitendinosus have a more powerful effect as hip extensors when the knee is straightened, while the rectus femoris can only flex the knee with full force if the knee joint is at the same time bent.

Rotators of the hip joint

External rotation Iliopsoas muscle	See above.
Gluteus maximus muscle	See above.
Rectus femoris muscle	See above.
Hip adductors	See above.
Internal rotation Tensor fasciae latae muscle	See above.
Part of the gluteus medius	See above.
Gracilis muscle	See above.

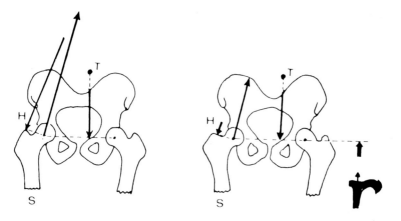

24   The load on the hip joint when the patient is standing on one leg (left) and when standing on one leg but supported by a stick in the opposite hand (right).
S = leg on which patient is standing; H = force applied by hip abductors; T = centre of gravity.
When the patient is standing on one leg, the hip joint bears a load equal to 2.5–3 times the body's weight, as a result of the unfavourable lever arm relationships. If a stick or crutch is used for support on the other side, then the load could in certain circumstances be reduced to about 10 kg.
After: Moritz 1975.

The functional mobility of the hip joint

For a normal sitting posture, one needs a hip flexion of 90°, and for standing up again, slightly more. When walking, one flexes the hip when swinging the leg by ca. 30°, and extends it in the standing phase to approximately 15°. When climbing stairs, approximately 50° of flexion in the hips is required, but when descending stairs, only about 10°. These values will of course depend on the height of the individual steps. In a normal gait, abduction and adduction movements require ca. 10–15°. When striding forwards, for example with the left leg, the left pelvis is rotated slightly forwards and the left femur is rotated outwards in the hip joint, whereas the right half of the pelvis rotates backwards and the right femur rotates relatively speaking inwards. An abduction position of both legs up to a malleolar distance of 70 cm and a certain measure of external rotation are preconditions for conventional sexual intercourse for a woman.

During walking, the hip joint is subjected to severe stress. The forces result from the weight of the body and the ratio of the lever arms. The lever arms have their origin in the midpoint of the head of the femur, and the lateral lever arm is limited by the insertion of the gluteus medius in the trochanter major and the bundle of tensors extending over the trochanter. The medial lever arm is at least 2½ times – and often up to 4 times – as long as the lateral lever arm, as a result of which stress on the hip joint can rise to three times the total body weight during the phase when all the weight is on one leg (Inman 1947, Frankel and Nordin 1980/**24**).

Experimental studies with implanted pressure gauges carried out during modern hip surgery have confirmed these values (Rydell 1966.)

The hip joint in inflammatory diseases of the joints

In chronic polyarthritis, one or in most cases both hips are affected in 15–40% of cases, depending on the series of examinations published. In ankylosing spondylitis, hip joints are affected in 50% of all cases, while the figure for juvenile chronic polyarthritis is 20%. In most cases there is a considerable tendency to contracture, with resulting deformity (Ansell 1980). The patient reacts to the severe hip pain which accompanies synovitis of this joint by seeking to relieve the pressure by shortening the length of the stress phase while walking and by shifting the centre of gravity and the upper part of the body to the same side. In this way, the centre of gravity can be shifted until it is directly above the hip joint. Thus, the pressure exercised as a result of the muscular traction can be considerably reduced. The strength of the stabilising hip abductors is limited by the pain. In time, they can atrophy to such a degree that they are no longer able to stabilise the pelvis when the patient is standing on one leg. We then have the positive Trendelenburg phenomenon. The same phenomenon can occur where there is severe destruction of the bony and cartilaginous parts of the hip joint. The distance between the origin and insertion of the hip abductors also shortens in many cases, so that their contraction force is correspondingly reduced.

It is important to recognise the danger of contracture in the hip region in good time, as physiotherapy can often achieve favourable results here. Contracture of the iliopsoas and the rectus occur very frequently in inflammatory diseases of the hips, and in ankylosing spondylitis, for example, they are frequently present at an early stage in the disease. In patients with juvenile chronic polyarthritis or chronic polyarthritis, contracture in the hip region can also lead to a chain reaction, with contractures occurring in the neighbouring joints. The lumbar spine is affected by hyperlordosis, which must be compensated by increased kyphosis of the thoracic spine and increased cervical lordosis, while the knee joint rapidly loses the ability to stretch. Hip and knee joint deformities severely affect the functional length of the leg, to which we shall return a little later on.

Flexion contracture of the hip joint is best examined with the patient lying down on the back with the opposite hip drawn up to the maximum extent, so that the lumbar lordosis is straightened up. Hip contractures should at all costs be treated to compensate the functional length of leg (see 'Contracture prophylaxis', p.103).

The knee joint

Anatomy and function
The knee joint is a complicated structure whose functional capability is largely determined by the shape of the joint surfaces, the state of the muscles and the remaining stabilising structures (Cailliet 1973). The joint surfaces of the femur and tibia enable the joint to be straightened out completely (0°) and flexed through more than 130°. Rotational movement is only possible with the knee slightly flexed, by about 5–10° in an inward direction, and by ca. 30–40° in an outward direction.

The following structures are involved in stabilising the knee joint:

• Cruciate ligament: the anterior cruciate ligament is tensioned during extension and in this position it prevents any outward rotation of the tibia. The posterior cruciate ligament stabilises the knee by preventing any shifting or luxation of the tibia towards the rear. It is tensioned when the knee joint is flexed and prevents rotation of the tibia inwards. The cruciate ligament is intra-articular, but extrasynovial.

• The collateral ligaments and iliotibial tract stabilise the knee joint medially and laterally.

• The quadriceps tendon stabilises the knee at the front.

• The gastrocnemius muscle and the capsule stabilise the joint at the rear.

Inadequate congruence of the joint surfaces is improved by a medial and a lateral meniscus. The two menisci are firmly united with the capsule and the intercondylar eminence. The various mucous bursae are also very important for the mobility of the knees. The most important are the suprapatellar bursa and the two infrapatellar bursae, one of which is deeply seated and the other closer to the surface, and which permit the patella to move by about 8–10 cm in a distal and proximal direction during flexion and extension of the knee. At the back of the knee is the bursa poplitea, which normally communicates with the knee.

Movements of the knee joint

Extension

Quadriceps femoris muscle, built up on the rectus femoris, vastus lateralis, vastus medialis and vastus intermedius	Extends from the pelvis and front surface of the femur in the form of a large ligament apparatus which contains the knee cap as sesamoid bone and is attached as the ligamentum patellae to the tubercle of the tibia.
Innervation:	Femoral nerve (L2–L4).

Flexion

Semimembranosus muscle	See hip joint.
Semitendinosus muscle	See hip joint.
Biceps femoris muscle	Originates as long head at the ischial tuberosity and as short head at the rear of the femur, extends to the head of the fibula and the tibia, and thus extends the hip joint and flexes the knee.
Innervation:	Sciatic nerve (L4–S2).
Gastrocnemius muscle	Extends from the lateral condyle and from the medial condyle down the calf and attaches to the posterior surface of the calcaneum as the Achilles tendon. This is the most powerful plantar flexor in the foot. If the foot is flat on the ground during walking or standing, then the gastrocnemius reacts on the knee joint as an extensor. If there is no quadriceps, the gastrocnemius can stabilise the foot, either during walking or standing when the foot is flat on the ground, in the terminal position of extension, working together with the hip extensors.
Innervation:	Medial popliteal nerve (L5–S2).

66

Function of the knee joint

In the normal knee joint, flexing causes the tibia surface to slide over the semicondyle towards the rear and at the same time to rotate slightly outwards, while the extension is accompanied by a slight rotation of the tibia in an inward direction. Extension of the knee joint takes place as a result of contraction of the quadriceps femoris muscle. The force is transmitted via the ligamentum patellae. An extending movement gives rise to considerable pressure between the joint surfaces of the femur and tibia, especially under load conditions, but also between the rear side of the patella and the upper front sections of the joint surface of the femur. Normal walking requires an amplitude of flexion of about 70° as a rule. When climbing stairs, a flexion of about 90° is required, with about 90–100° for descending stairs. Sitting in an armchair requires a flexion of 110°, while riding a bicycle calls for 100° flexion.

The stress on the knee joint will depend on the body weight of the individual and on the angle at which this weight acts on the joint surfaces. Getting up from a low chair gives an intra-articular compression force 5–6 times the body weight, according to calculations made by Ellis *et al.* (1979).

The knee joint in inflammatory diseases of the joints

In chronic polyarthritis, synovitis with exudation occurs in at least 60% of all cases. The synovitis spreads round the inside of the capsule, following the blood vessels, attacks the cruciate ligaments and menisci, moves on to the joint cartilage and can also attack all the other parts of the joint, especially the recessus superior. The pain caused by the inflammation under load conditions can easily lead to the patient taking up a more flexed position than physiologically necessary. In the flexed position, the joint cavity is at its widest, the pressure applied by the joint fluid is relatively speaking at its lowest and the pain can then be kept to the minimum. In addition, the patient will reduce the load phase to the minimum. This inhibition of pain and the inadequate loading of the joint will result, with practically all diseases of the knee joint but especially with arthritis, in an extraordinarily rapid onset of atrophy, in this case of the quadriceps. Exudation, expansion of the capsule, muscle wasting and loss of cartilage substance mean a loss of stability in the knee joint, both in the flexed and in the extended position.

In ankylosing spondylitis, the knee joint in young boys and adolescents shows the first signs of attack in many cases. In juvenile

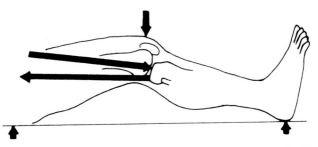

25 **When the knee joint is passively straightened by pressure applied from the outside,** considerable traction forces arise as a result of the leverage, for example at the rear capsule. At the same time, the joint surfaces are pressed together with the same force. The length of the arrow is proportional to the size of the forces (Moritz 1975).

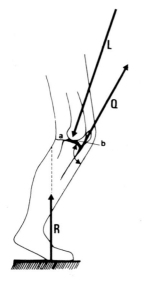

Loading of the knee joint when standing with different values of extension deficit (Perry 1967).

Extension deficit	Joint loading
10°	1.01 × body weight
20°	1.20 × body weight
30°	1.60 × body weight
40°	2.60 × body weight

26 **Loading conditions in the knee joint with failure of extension.**
R = reaction force (body weight), a = lever arm on which the reaction force acts, Q = quadriceps force, b = lever arm of this force. The joint surfaces were selected as the point of application of the moments of force. The length of the arrows is proportional to the forces which arise. In a static state of equilibrium, $R \times a = Q + b$. If b is smaller than a, then Q is greater than R. If a increases (i.e. the extension deficit), then the intra-articular stress will also increase. The joint loading (L) in total is a function of R and Q (Moritz 1975).

chronic polyarthritis, ca. 60% of all cases involved arthritis in the knee joint, and here too, it was often the first manifestation of the disease.

Subluxation to the rear and flexion contracture
Synovitides can easily lead to instability in the joint, either via the mechanism of stretching and destroying the stabilising soft part apparatus or through destruction of cartilage and bone. If flexion contracture develops, the capsule and the flexor tendons at the back of the knee joint will shrink, so that the normal forward slide of the tibia is prevented. This results in characteristic damage to the joint cartilage of the femur condyle. In all, the result is a subluxation position towards the rear. Unfortunately, damage to the joint may also result from incorrect physical treatment of a flexion contracture (Brattström *et al.* 1971/25).

Synovitides can also spread to the bursae in the knee cavity. If the joint cavity contains fluid, this will be extended into the bursa when the knee is bent, but can no longer flow back into the cavity when the knee is extended again, owing to the valve mechanism which is set up. As a result, the popliteal bursae occasionally increase in volume and become known as popliteal cysts, or Baker's cysts. On occasions such a cyst tracks down into the lower leg and in the event of rupture, can simulate all the symptoms of an acute venous thrombosis. Baker's cysts hinder mobility and often accentuate existing contractures.

A knee with a flexion contracture of 20–30° must stand 1.6 times the body's weight when the individual is standing, because the centre of gravity in this case is behind the axis of movement (**26**). When climbing stairs, the patient can compensate for the resulting imbalance by leaning forwards. This makes climbing stairs easier and less painful than descending them, when the weight of the body must be taken up although the centre of gravity lies behind the joint. Frequently, the problem is solved by the patient descending stairs backwards.

Valgus deformities
Knee damage in chronic polyarthritis generally affects the lateral part of the joint and thereby causes valgus deformities (Deane 1970). However, a thorough examination should in any case be made to see whether any deformity is not primarily due to adduction or inner rotation contracture in the hip joint or primarily caused by deformities in the region of the tarsal bones or the metatarsus. It is often the case that all these joints or groups of joints are affected at the same time, and in such instances the possible interactions must also be

taken into consideration. More rarely, varus deformities may be found, but these are more typical of gonarthrosis.

The onset of any lateral instability should be carefully watched for: surgical intervention to protect the joint will have a better chance of success if it is undertaken before any significant lateral instability has arisen, and while the cruciate ligaments are still reasonably intact. If an endoprosthesis is required, stability is a decisive factor in the selection of the most suitable type. In order to achieve satisfactory long-term results, it is important to correct the angle of loading.

The onset of ankylosing spondylitis and juvenile chronic polyarthritis in the knee joints is characterised by a tendency to contracture. Instability is less common. When the body is growing, synovitis can lead to an acceleration of growth in the affected leg or to a premature closing of the epiphysis, thus decreasing final stature in the extremity concerned, so that different lengths of leg occur (Brattström and Sundberg 1965/ see also 'Gait and length of leg', p.74). Pain in the knee joints can also be caused by inflammation of the tendon sheaths at the back of the joint or by a bursitis pedis anserini or by a synovitis in the fibulotibial joint. Here again, there is a risk of contracture.

Taking a long-term view, it is important to eliminate at an early stage any factor which could lead to instability or contracture of the knee joint. Synovitides which do not respond to antiphlogistic treatment, must at all costs be eliminated by means of synovectomy, either chemical or surgical. Contractures which resist treatment can be corrected by means of tenotomy and/or posterior capsulotomy, or by lateral release (Goldie 1975).

The foot and its joints

Anatomy and function

The foot and its joints serve to support the entire weight of the body and are of paramount importance for locomotion (Cailliet 1968, Kirkup 1974).

From a functional point of view, the foot can be broken down as follows:

1 The calcaneal part of the foot, together with the ankle joint and calcaneus.
2 The metatarsus, consisting of the navicular bone, cuneiform bones, cuboid bone and metatarsal bones.
3 The forefoot with metatarsophalangeal joints and toes.

The ankle joint is a hinge-like joint with dorsoplantar mobility. It is made up of the trochlea of the talus and the joint surfaces of the tibia and fibula. The upper joint surface of the talus forms a joint with the tibia, the two joint surfaces to the side, lateral and medial, form joints with the joint surfaces of the malleoli.

The stability of the ankle is at its greatest when the foot forms an angle of 90° with the lower leg. The joint surfaces of the talus are narrower towards the back and form a gap when the foot is plantar-flexed, e.g. when high heels are worn. On the underside of the talus there are three joint surfaces, which form joints with the calcaneus, forming the talocalcanear joint, or lower part of the ankle joint. This includes the connections between the talus and the navicular and between the calcaneus and cuboid bones.

Further down, the navicular bone, the cuneiform bones I–III and the cuboid bone meet the metatarsal bones. The stability of these joints is normally very good. They make supination and inversion (adduction) of the foot possible on the one hand, and pronation and eversion (abduction) on the other.

When the ankle joint is loaded, the body weight is transmitted from the tibia to the talus, which is pushed forward medially in the process. At the same time, the calcaneus slides forward, so that the joint takes on a slight valgus position. The plantar aponeurosis, the very powerful ligaments and the intrinsic muscles stabilise the foot while under load conditions.

The articular system of the forefoot has particular dorsal mobility, owing to the shape of the joint surfaces. This is of the greatest importance for walking in a heel-to-toe fashion. Under normal conditions, the spreading action, and the abduction and adduction, are of no significance.

The tibia and fibula are held together by a powerful interosseous apparatus of ligaments. Collateral ligaments which come from the malleoli, stabilise the bones of the foot and the subtalar joints. Medially, the deltoid ligament in particular is involved, extending from the tip of the tibia to the navicular bone and the talus, while laterally, there are the ligaments which extend from the tip of the fibula to the talus (ligamentum fibulotalare anterius and posterius) and to the calcaneus.

One can therefore describe the foot in terms of a system with three arches stabilised by the interosseous ligaments and muscles.

- a longitudinal arch consisting of talus, calcaneus, navicular bone, cuneiform I and metatarsal I.

- a proximal transverse arch consisting of cuneiformia I–III and cuboid bone.

- a distal transverse arch consisting of the distal ends of the metatarsalia.

Deformities of the feet are extremely common, even in otherwise healthy people, so there is an enormous variety of foot shapes.

Foot muscles

The foot muscles too, can be divided up into extrinsic muscles which originate from the leg and have their insertion in the foot, and intrinsic muscles, which have both their origin and insertion in the foot.

The most powerful of the plantar flexors is the triceps surae, which starts in two places: the epicondyle of the femur (gastrocnemius) and the rear surface of the proximal tibia (the soleus muscle). The muscle attaches itself, by means of a single tendon, the Achilles tendon, to the posterior surface of the calcaneum. The triceps surae acts both on the ankle and on the knee joint. The tone of the triceps muscles stabilises the body when standing, when the centre of gravity lies in front of the talus. It is also involved in the final phase of the movement, rocking on the ball of the foot.

The extrinsic muscles at the front of the foot (tibialis anterior, extensor hallucis longus, extensor digitorum longus) cause dorsal flexion and inversion of the ankle, while the peronei (fibulares) muscles are responsible for plantar flexion and eversion. The two groups of muscles together have a stabilising effect and are also active in standing. The intrinsic muscles, together with the powerful tissue structures of the plantar fasciae, have a predominantly stabilising function. The muscles of the leg are mainly innervated by the medial popliteal nerve (L5–S2).

Function of the ankle

For walking on an even surface, the ankle requires a range of movement of about 40°, as well as metatarsophalangeal joints with dorsal mobility. Eversion and inversion capability are also required. This is even more necessary when walking on an uneven surface. Climbing stairs calls for about 10–15° of movement, while descending stairs calls for more extension in the ankle.

The foot in inflammatory diseases of the joints

In chronic polyarthritis, the foot is almost always involved, while in ankylosing spondylitis this is rare, and the function of the feet is more likely to be impaired by synovitides in the region of the ankles, the tarsal joints and the metatarsophalangeal joints. Inflammatory changes can lead to stretching of the tendons and ligaments and can cause painful reactions. Owing to the great amount of stress to which the feet are subjected, a general instability of the entire complex structure can occur, resulting in deformities (Vidigal *et al.* 1975, Cailliet 1968, Dixon and Kates 1970, Tillman 1979). The gait changes in a characteristic way, due to the pain caused by the synovitides in the intertarsal and metatarsophalangeal joints: the weight is shifted on to the heels or on to the whole foot in an unphysiological manner, the foot is no longer rolled from heel to toe, and the steps taken become shorter. Such movement requires only little activity on the part of the quadriceps and the rest of the leg and foot muscles are only used to a limited extent as well, so that pronounced weakness and atrophy of the muscles results. Synovitides in the metarsophalangeal joints mostly result in the big toe adopting the valgus position (see below). As a result of destruction and dorsal luxation of the proximal phalanges, the other toes also become unstable, so that in the end, hammer toes or clawfoot and painful callosities occur. This development is also furthered by the powerful traction of the diseased ligaments.

Pes valgus
The valgus position is the most common deformity of the ankle and is functionally connected with corresponding variants of knee and possibly hip shapes (Kirkup 1974). Rheumatic pes valgus arises because of arthritis and instability of the talonavicular and calcaneocuboid joints, but also in part as a result of subtalar and talocrural instability and lateral displacement of the heel-bone. The fork slides forward and towards the middle, colliding with the calcaneus and giving rise to pain in the tip of the fibula.

In patients with long-standing flexion contractures of the knee joint or with significant differences in the lengths of the legs, dropfoot (fixed plantar flexion) frequently occurs. Varus positions of the calcaneal part of the foot are occasionally found in children, but are very rare in the adult rheumatic.

Hallux valgus
The big toe has one phalanx fewer than the other toes. The first metatarsophalangeal joint therefore has a special role in the heel-to-toe movement of the foot (Jacoby *et al.* 1976). On the plantar side of the big toe are a lateral and medial sesamoid bone, embedded in the flexor tendons. They take an active part in the stabilisation of the basal joint. Synovitides in the basal joint of the big toe lead to lateral displacement of this tendon, and the corresponding muscle then acts as an adductor – if we take a line through the middle cluster as our

point of reference. The intrinsic muscle of the big toe, the adductor hallucis, pulls in the same direction and is not compensated in terms of stability by the abductor hallucis on the medial side of the first cluster. The big toe deviates correspondingly to the side, and adopts a valgus position. This deformity is found in the majority of chronic polyarthritic patients. In most cases, there is simultaneous development of inflammatory flatfoot with broadening of the feet, due to destruction of the ligaments between the tarsal bone and the ossea metatarsalia.

Hallux rigidus
Stiffening of the metatarsophalangeal joints with restriction of extension in the region of the big toe are often partial symptoms of hallux valgus, but can also occur on their own. The cause is to be found in a synovitis with a tendency to stiffening in the basal joint of the big toe. Hyperextension or a valgus position of the interphalangeal joint can develop by way of compensation.

Arthritides in the lateral toes can easily destabilise the forefoot, and can lead to the development of hammer toes and clawfoot, or to multiple accretions of horny skin. Sclerosis under the third metatarsal head is especially typical (centre forward callosity).

It is quite possible that the primary reaction to pain and the resulting pattern adopted by each individual to relieve the strain on the feet determines the development of foot deformities. If one puts one's weight on the inside of the foot in order to relieve localised pain on the lateral side, then a pes valgus or hallux valgus can easily develop. If the weight is placed on the outside edge of the foot in order to relieve a painful big toe, then there will be a predominant tendency to stiffening and occasionally to flexion deformity of the basal joint of the big toe. Rheumatic inflammation of the tendon sheaths of the tibialis and fibularis muscles is frequent. In many cases, thickening of the tendon sheath tissues under the ligamentum laciniatum can lead to compression of the medial popliteal nerve behind the medial malleolus. Symptoms may appear in the foot which correspond to the carpal tunnel syndrome in the hand.

Gait and length of leg

In patients with chronic polyarthritis in the lower extremities, no examination is complete without a thorough analysis of the patient's gait. This will frequently give an impression of the nature and location of the changes, and whether they merely cause pain or also restrict the patient's movements. It is best to watch the patient walk down a long

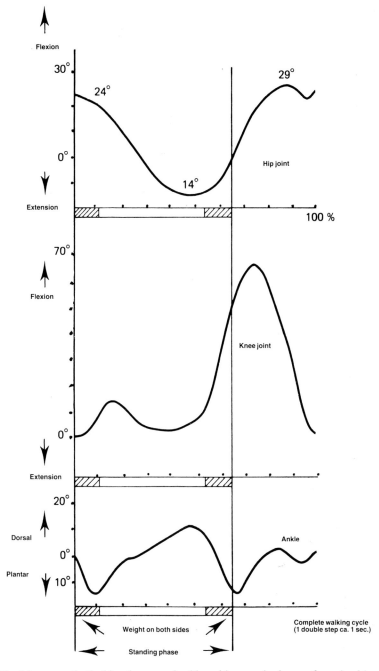

27 Movement in the hips, knees and ankles with normal gait, seen from the side.

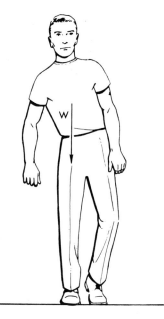

28 Duchenne phenomenon in case of pain in the hip joint. The weight of the upper part of the body and thus the centre of gravity, is transferred over the pivot of the joint to relieve the pain in the hip.
After: Williams and Lissner: Biomechanics of Human Motion, W.B.Saunders Co., 1962.

corridor, or across a large room. Watching the patient climbing stairs is also part of the examination, as well as coming down again, sitting down on a normal chair and standing up again, and if possible climbing up on to a chair.

The normal gait has a very complex pattern of movements which demand a normal neurological status with normal deep and superficial sensibility, normal motor functions, normal coordination and a completely pain-free support and locomotion apparatus. The gait can conveniently be divided up into two phases, the standing and swinging phases. Normally, both legs are stressed at the same time for a brief moment during walking (27/Eberhardt and Inman 1966).

Locomotion disorders in rheumatic patients
Many rheumatic patients suffer from locomotion disorders, stemming from a wide variety of causes (Moritz and Svantesson 1970).

As a result of synovitis in one or more weight-bearing joints, pain is experienced by the patient which disturbs the normal pattern when walking, since the patient is involuntarily seeking to stress the painful joints for as short a period as possible. As a result, the patient walks in a position in which pain can be kept to a minimum (28).

With painful arthritis of the hip, the patient will begin to limp, shortening the time the painful joint is stressed and reducing the forces compressing it. The latter is achieved by shifting the body weight, or more precisely the line of gravity, vertically through the

76

affected joint. The patient inclines the upper part of the body in the standing phase to the same side as the painful hip.

Painful hip joints are kept in a slightly flexed position under load conditions, and as a result secondary contractures and deformities of the hip and ankle often develop.

In arthritis of the back part of the foot, the forefoot as a rule takes the weight, and the ankle is kept more or less rigid, with the foot mainly turned outwards and rolled medially over the ankle. In such cases, the knee joint is often kept in a slightly flexed position, which accelerates the occurrence of flexion contracture in the knee joint.

In flexion contractures of the hip joint, the length of pace of the sound leg is also affected, the steps become shorter and the full extension of the healthy hip joint can no longer be used. When rotation at the hip is no longer possible, a screw-like gait develops. Inadequate extension in the diseased hip joints can in part be compensated by hyperlordosis of the lumbar spine. Patients with a stiff spine do not have this possibility and disabilities of this sort are clearly recognisable. Hip joints with contracture of the abductors or adductors and simultaneous flexion contracture of the knee joint lead to differences, functional or real, in the length of the legs. Flexion contractures of the knee joints or dropfoot deformities lead to a marked shortening of the length of steps. Instability affects the pattern of the gait as well. With valgus deformities, this can be particularly grotesque. These patients walk with very small steps, often with a screwing action at the knees, and attempt to compensate for the instability by pressing the thighs and knees together.

Differences in length of legs
A difference in the length of the legs can develop in rheumatic patients for quite different reasons. We must first differentiate between real and apparent differences in length.

Real differences in length
Children with arthritis of the knee joint can experience a stimulation of skeletal growth in the region of the growth zone as a result of hyperaemia, so that the affected leg could grow 2–4 cm longer than the healthy one. On the other hand, the arthritic process can prematurely bring growth to a halt.

Real differences in the length of the legs can also be found as a result of destruction in the hip or knee joints or after knee joint resection and arthrodesis. In all these cases, the longer leg is not fully stretched when walking and increasingly adopts a valgus position. As a result, the pattern of gait is characteristically altered. In many cases, the

29 Compensation mechanisms for different lengths of leg after knee joint arthrodesis.

patient compensates for the difference by plantar flexion of the shorter leg and walks on the toes (Brattström and Brattström 1971/**29**).

Apparent differences

A functional shortening of a leg is a frequent occurrence and is caused above all by contracture in weight-bearing joints. In abduction contractures of the hip, the affected leg appears to be too long from a functional point of view, while in adduction contractures, it appears to be too short. In both cases, the pathological inclination of the pelvis represents the actual functional damage. In the same way, flexion contracture in the knee joint and footdrop are causes of functional differences in length of leg. Apparent differences are mainly compensated in the same way as actual differences: the longer leg is flexed at the knee and kept in a slight valgus position, or the foot is hardly rolled at all. Patients with ankylosing spondylitis frequently compensate with the spine, which can then ossify in a pronounced scoliosis.

It is extremely important for future treatment to determine whether any difference in length of leg is functional or real.

Analysis of differences in length of leg

It is extremely important to check the mobility of hip and knee joints. If they can move freely, then one can determine the real length of leg from the spina iliaca anterior superior to the tip of the medial malleolus. Such measurements must be made with the patient lying flat on his back, with both legs exactly parallel to the body axis.

Examination of standing patient

Whether the pelvis is horizontal and whether it is rotated in any way or not, is best determined with the patient standing up. For this purpose, one can use a special spirit level with two lever arms which are placed on the rim of the pelvis. If the pelvis is inclined, then carefully graduated pieces of wood are placed under the short leg until the pelvis has reached a horizontal position. The total thickness of wood placed under the shorter leg then represents the real or functional difference in length of leg. If a functional difference is due to abduction or adduction contracture in the hip, it is of course not possible to bring the pelvis to a horizontal position.

Treatment of differences in length of leg
Usually only real differences in the length of leg should be compensated by increasing the height of heels and thickness of soles. With rheumatic patients who have problems with their feet it is unacceptable to increase only the height of the heel, as the extension in the heel is reduced as a result and overstressing of the forefoot can lead to increased pain. Functional differences, such as shortening due to adduction contracture in the hip, should be corrected by appropriate treatment, possibly by adductortenotomy. Any increase here in the height of heel or thickness of sole would merely increase the extent of the existing deformity.

Day-to-day activities

In order to be able to devise a realistic plan of treatment, it is first necessary to determine what the patient's functional capabilities are in terms of the usual day-to-day activities. For this, the physiotherapist must get to know the patient's surroundings personally. To draw up the necessary report, we routinely visit the patients in their homes, and in certain cases we also visit their place of work. One can of course obtain a reasonable impression from an interview, but appearances can be deceptive and the results are rarely so satisfactory, as many handicapped patients underestimate their own capabilities. Very often they have relations who are able and willing to lend a hand on demand. Other patients overestimate their own abilities and are unwilling to admit, either to themselves or to those around them, the seriousness of the problems facing them. A practical test in their own surroundings is the best foundation for planning the therapy, irrespective of whether it is a question of trying out technical aids, adapting the home to the changed requirements brought about by the condition, or preparatory to an operation. With rheumatic sufferers, their specific condition can change from hour to hour. The morning is a particularly bad time.

The report on activities of daily living covers the following headings:

Clothing and hygiene

- Dressing and undressing upper and lower parts of the body unaided.

- Dental hygiene.

- Hygiene, upper and lower parts of the body.

- Leg and foot hygiene: these are particularly important, since as a result of arthritis in the small joints of the feet, painful callosities can form on the affected toes. Prophylactic treatment presents the best protection against infection. See also Part II 'Joint protection'.

- Visiting the toilet and feminine hygiene, including tampons and contraceptive aids.

Daily activities requiring use of the hands to a decisive extent

- Make-up.

- Care of nails.

- Sewing.

- Knitting, embroidery, etc.

- Writing.

- Cutting with scissors.

Getting about (mobility)

- Rising from a lying to a sitting position.

- Standing up from a sitting position.

- Walking on a smooth floor.

- Climbing stairs, negotiating door sills (state height of steps).

- Getting into and out of cars, buses, trains or other public transport, possibly use of a special vehicle for the handicapped (Chamberlain and Buchanan 1977).

- Driving a car.

- Use of walking aids.

Activities in the home

- Cooking: range or cooker, taps, pots and pans. Cutting, pouring, stirring and beating.

- Clearing up and dusting: washing up, hoovering, brushing, wiping.

- Hobbies: gardening, sewing, crocheting, knitting, playing cards, etc.

- Occupation, profession.

- Living together.

There are many forms that can be used to record all the necessary details of day-to-day activities. The interview itself can be extremely frustrating for the patient, particularly if severely handicapped, so the therapist must be careful to determine not only the things that the patient cannot do, but also those that he or she can do without help, in order to create as positive an atmosphere as possible. It is an advantage to use a separate form for each class of function. Alternatively, one could allow the patient to fill in a standardised form for himself whenever a call is made to check progress, so as to get a more comprehensive list of activities (Lee *et al.* 1973, Fries 1980).

Analysis of day-to-day activities
Day-to-day activities are generally complicated patterns composed of a large number of tiny elements. It is important to analyse the overall picture in order to be able to pick out the details which can be changed.

Examples:

The inability to eat without assistance
The following barriers to normal function are possible:

- Stiffness and pain through synovitis in the shoulder joint.

- Pain and loss of flexion in the elbow.

- Painful wrist joint.

- Inability to close the hand up or clench the fist due to swan neck deformity.

- Weakness and instability of the fingers due to mutilating changes in the bones.

- Unstable thumb.

- Inability to open the mouth properly due to restricted movement in ankylosing spondylitis or juvenile chronic polyarthritis.

Treatment should be specifically directed towards the particular condition: pains in the shoulder are treated, for example, by intra-articular administration of corticosteroid preparations or synovectomy of the shoulder joint. For the elbow, the same treatment could be used, or plastic surgery. Impaired functions of the hand can partly be helped by the use of technical aids, for example a painful and unstable wrist can be stabilised by fitting an individually designed brace. Another method of stabilisation would be arthrodesis.

Causes of inability to use the toilet unaided
The causes of this problem could lie with either the upper or the lower extremities. There may be insufficient flexion in the hips, pain in the knees or weakness in the hip and knee muscles which make it impossible for the patient to sit down or stand up unaided. Deformities in the region of the joints of the upper extremities may make it difficult for the patient to wipe himself properly.

Other factors, such as a poor bathroom layout, or too low a toilet seat, could also rob the patient of independence in this respect.

No doubt improvements with regard to such functions could be brought about by local administration of corticosteroid preparations or by synovectomy. On the other hand, by adapting the existing facilities, for example, by fitting a raised toilet seat or installing a Closomat which replaces the function of the upper extremities, the problems can be alleviated to a considerable extent. The essential precondition for any such specific measure is a careful study of the problem and of the surroundings and facilities, before taking the simplest and most practical solution and implementing it.

The home
The difficulties experienced by a handicapped person in his everyday life can depend very largely on the home surroundings. A visit to the home can therefore throw much light on the demands the home makes on the patient. At the same time, one has an opportunity to make contact with spouses, family, friends and helpers who may become involved with the patient.

In the home, one should carefully observe the various tasks that are performed and how they are performed and establish which operations place an unnecessary strain on the joints or are uneconomic in terms of effort expended. All the tools, implements and gadgets used should be light and practical. In this way, the instruction given to patients in the protection of their joints will be more realistic and appropriate, and can be adapted to their own specific problems.

The following should be noted on visiting the home:

- Kitchen and kitchen equipment, including taps.

- Bath and toilet, including taps.

- Laundering, ironing, care of clothes.

- Chairs, day beds, beds.

- Door handles and knobs on cupboards, windows.

- Stairs and staircases, lifts, door sills, corridors, doors.

- Entrances and exits, path to rubbish bin.

- Distance to shops and public transport. Whether car is available.

Should a home visit be impossible, such details could be taken down in the occupational therapy department or in a mobile centre.

Psychological assessment

Crises and reaction to crises

If a normal healthy person is suddenly struck down by a serious illness, an accident or by the loss of someone particularly dear, then he or she is faced with a crisis. As we know from established patterns, this leads from a state of shock and depression to one in which the patient seeks to readjust and re-orient himself to his changed situation. Crisis situations can serve to mature an individual and contribute to the further development of his personality, but can also lead to regression if the individual is unwilling to accept the new situation. There are many reasons to believe that a diagnosis of chronic polyarthritis amounts to a crisis situation, with corresponding reactions. It is conceivable that part of the symptoms in the advanced stages of the disease are the result of insufficient 'digestion' of the problems posed in the early stages. (Cullberg 1976, Baker 1981, Baum 1982, Kaij 1974, Kiviniemi 1977, Rimon 1969, 1984, Robinson *et al.* 1971.)

Depression and tiredness

The rheumatism sufferer is often tired and weary and we must do our very best to find out what the real cause is. The inflammatory disease itself with the accompanying anaemia, but also some of the medications prescribed for the disease, can cause fatigue.

A true depressive reaction shows as a change in daily rhythms. Such patients find it difficult to get to sleep at night, and difficult to get going again in the morning, are uninterested, lack appetite and seem to have lost vitality. The depression is an expression of their concern and of the helpless rage they feel about their situation. Often the patients are scarcely aware of their depression. After long years of suffering, the depression may be hidden behind a smile of resignation. Patients also learn to put their worries out of their minds (disguised depression).

Depressed patients have greatly reduced self-confidence and often find it very difficult to carry out the training programme set out for them, e.g. after operations. Many doctors therefore see depression as a contraindication to surgical intervention. Treatment with appropriate drugs, such as thymoleptics, in conjunction with psychotherapy, can do a great deal to relieve the depressive reactions.

Profiting from the disease

With chronic diseases of the joints, the extent to which the sufferer is dependent on those around him is often all too obvious. Occasionally, however, a submissive and self-destructive person can tyrannise everyone in his surroundings with his demands for help, support and attention, to an extent quite unwarranted by his incapacity. This sort of behaviour is the expression of a neurotic personality which makes it extremely difficult or even quite impossible for the individual to come to terms with the realities of the situation. The description of emotional reactions to chronic diseases shows how important it is to obtain a clear picture of how the patient has managed to cope with the crisis brought on by the disease, i.e. whether he has accepted the situation and whether he could take a realistic part in discussions on the nature and objectives of various methods of treatment.

Adaptation to the disease in this context is the 'honest reaction', in which the patient recognises that the disease will not go away again, but in which he also sees those aspects of his life which are not affected by the disease and consciously decides to concentrate on them. A patient who has learned to accept his disease will not harbour unrealistic expectations with regard to treatment. In addition, the course usually taken by the disease makes the patient's situation that much more difficult, since each deterioration calls for a new effort of adjustment.

Family circumstances

Severe illness can cause difficulties in a marriage and in the family, and can also lead to problems of a sexual nature (Currey 1970, Erlich 1973*a*, Nordquist 1984, Rimon 1969, 1984, Stewart 1975, Wright 1976). Inflammatory diseases of the joints do not affect the sex organs as such, but pain on movement, stiffness, depression, tiredness and a reduced sense of one's own worth can play havoc with the libido. This is particularly true during the active phases of the disease.

The present day tendency to glorify 'the body beautiful' makes it more difficult for the arthritic patient to accept his disease. Hands afflicted with active synovitides and deformed fingers are seen as ugly and unfit for loving. Stiffened hips and knees with contractures change one's appearance and make it difficult to use the classical positions for love-making. One's changed attitude toward one's body can lead to feelings of inferiority. It often takes a long time to accept that, if one does not have a partner with whom one can work it all out. For the partner too, it is often a great help if the patient speaks about his reactions to the new situation. The need to discuss at length the problems arising in order to defuse them and even to overcome them altogether is something that doctors and therapists have so far paid too little attention to.

Social background

In addition to the patient's own maturity and emotional stability, there are a number of other possibilities which could help him to master the situation.

The family
There is a constant demand for the family of patients to be involved in the continual rehabilitation. This means that the spouse, or the parents or the children must have a knowledge of the disease and of the possible aids. The most important factor in this is that they should all have mastered their own reactions to the disease. Many helpers learn very quickly about the disease and its treatment. Many healthy people, however, would not like to admit to having such a disease in their surroundings. With children, fear and uncertainty about the disease could at worst mean that they turn against the patient. The whole situation within the family and how the disease can affect relationships needs more attention and investigation than has so far been given to it.

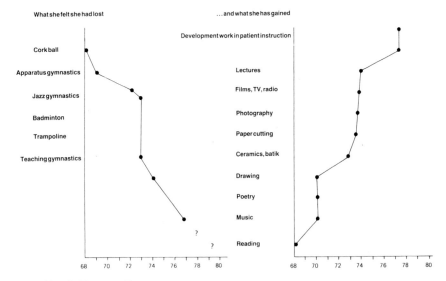

What she felt she had lost ... and what she has gained

Development work in patient instruction

Cork ball
Apparatus gymnastics   Lectures
Jazz gymnastics   Films, TV, radio
Badminton   Photography
Trampoline   Paper cutting
Teaching gymnastics   Ceramics, batik
                                    Drawing
                                    Poetry
                                    Music
                        ?   Reading

30 A 32 year old teacher describes how her situation has changed since she developed chronic polyarthritis. Every lost function, every restriction was countered with a new stage in personal development. In her opinion, her life overall has been enriched, in spite of it all (Heramb 1982).

Training and occupation

In occupations which do not make heavy demands on patients in terms of mobility or energy expenditure, it is often possible to re-integrate them into the working community. In many cases, it requires new social contacts. Training already received can be expanded, so as to put off the day when the patient is no longer able to pursue his occupation.

Circle of friends and hobbies

Man has the capability to develop in many directions and in most cases, only a very small part of our talents are actually used. A disease such as arthritis can force one to take a closer look at one's interests, to drop some and take up others, so that the quality of life will not inevitably deteriorate. As therapists, it is our duty to help the patient in this respect too. The diagram (**30**) shows how an increase in the number of interests can lead to a larger circle of friends, and thus a fuller life.

Part II

Joint protection

As described in detail in Part I, inflammatory diseases affect the whole being. One important general problem is the tiredness the patient feels, particularly when the disease is active. Local problems include pains in the joints, weakness, instability and deformities. Measures taken to dampen down the activity and thus ease the pain and the tiredness, and those which lead to reduction of stress on joints and muscles, have the effect of protecting the joints. Changes in the psychosocial situation and the patient's milieu in the widest sense can also lead indirectly to relief. Different aspects of the treatment, such as local steroid injections, suitably adapted technical aids, a suitable home, good means of transport etc. are all links in the chain of the programme of treatment whose sole purpose is to protect the joints against unnecessary stress and uneconomic use of the patient's limited resources. For the rheumatic sufferer, protecting his joints means rethinking and retraining to prepare for a different way of life, which he must maintain even on his better days. It goes without saying that the family must be involved.

Changing and adapting calls for motivation. The therapist must therefore establish to what extent the patient has accepted his disease. If he has not accepted it or come to terms with it, motivation is lacking, and he will not be receptive to new information (see Patient Instruction Sheets, p.212-234). Protection of the joints presupposes that the patient knows how articular functions can be maintained and improved:

- by daily contracture prophylaxis,

- by a suitably adapted way of life and avoidance of stress,

- by using technical aids,

- by using orthoses.

The cervical spine

Immobilisation, physiotherapy

Neck supports in the form of soft surgical collars or plastic collars (Plastazote) specially fitted to the neck and the nape of the neck alleviate the pain in the neck and at the same time provide the required degree of restriction of movement (Althoff, Goldie 1980). It does not completely immobilise the neck, as the functional X-ray with the support in place shows. However, this measure does draw the attention of the patient to the cervical neck again. In individual, severe cases it may be necessary to lock the head in position by means of a special collar, with screws to adjust the required position.

If the cervical spine is affected with instability of the atlanto-occipital joint which shows up on an X-ray, the patient must be carefully briefed about his condition and the symptoms that would indicate any deterioration.

Pain in the nape of the neck can be treated with some success by massage and careful traction, with the patient lying down. Traction is contraindicated in the case of instability, and when it gives rise to pain. X-ray examination should always be carried out before undertaking such treatment. When sitting down, the patient frequently finds relief from a neck support on the chair or wheelchair. Any position in which the head is tilted forwards should be avoided, as this would increase the symptoms and there would also be the risk of compression of the spinal cord. A reading desk would be very welcome as a supplementary aid, with automatic page turning for those with especially weak upper extremities.

All rheumatic patients whose cervical spine is affected should avoid using seat belts when travelling in cars, for a sudden braking when the upper part of the body is restrained could lead to sudden flexion in the area of the neck, with fatal results.

When lying down, the patient whose cervical spine is affected should use a soft collar to support the head and use a small cushion as well to fill out the lordosis in the neck. In many cases, the pain in the neck can be very severe, and massage of the neck muscles by a physiotherapist or a specially trained relative or helper would be helpful. Occasionally, heat treatment can alleviate the discomfort, while isolated patients benefit from transcutaneous electrostimulation, though so far we have not been able to gather much information or experience on the subject.

If trouble with the neck persists in spite of the treatments described, or if any neurological symptoms become more pronounced, the possibility of an operation to fix the position of the unstable segment of the cervical spine should be considered (Brattström and Granholm 1976, Awerbuch et al. 1981, Kataoka et al. 1979). Before any surgical intervention under anaesthetic is undertaken on a rheumatism patient, it is absolutely essential to examine the cervical neck and take note of any instability in the neck; failure to do so would amount to inexcusable neglect.

With ankylosing spondylitis patients, the daily contracture prophylaxis which commences after the diagnosis will contribute in the long term to a delay in the stiffening of the cervical spine and at the same time will help to enable any unavoidable fixing of the head to be achieved at least in a comfortable position.

Any cushions used by ankylosing spondylitis patients should be as small as possible. However, in spite of the most intensive prophylaxis, it is often impossible to prevent stiffening of the neck. Any problems experienced when driving cars can be reduced by means of suitable auxiliary mirrors.

Summary:

Joint protection in the cervical spine

- Best possible position of patient.

- Traction and massage after X-ray.

- Neither manipulation nor muscle training on rheumatic necks.

- Head support when seated, and reading desk if required.

- No safety belts in cars.

- Careful contracture prophylaxis in ankylosing spondylitis.

Upper extremities

Contracture prophylaxis

Motto: 'Prevention is better than cure' applies to deformities too!

A programme of therapy aimed at preventing contracture is the foundation of any system of joint protection. Pain in the joints caused by synovitis can be treated with intra-articular steroid injections. With pain and restriction of mobility due to increased friction resistance, e.g. due to tenosynovitides, the injection is given in the point of the attachment of the tendon or in the connective tissue surrounding the tendons. Contracture prophylaxis is best carried out in a relaxed state, and should not give rise to any pain. Pain is in any case a warning signal, which should be respected, analysed and acted on. Exercises under low load conditions are best carried out in a warm water bath (34–35°C), but exercises on a sling table are also suitable.

In planning a programme for the individual patient, it is important to know how much mobility and how much strength the patient needs to be able to cope with the day-to-day running of the home and at work.

The thoracic girdle
(For anatomy and function, see p.31.)

Exercises for contracture prophylaxis of the shoulders are carried out under no-load conditions, either lying down on a bed with the arms resting on the bed, or standing up but inclined slightly forwards, in the form of pendular movements, possibly with a light weight in the hands. A further alternative for exercises of the shoulder joints under no-load conditions is provided by the sling table. The patient can make his own sling support or have it made for him, using a simple block and pulley, and use it every day to take the weight of the arms while exercising. The best method which provides the maximum relief for the joints and maximum scope for movement is again the warm water bath.

During contracture prophylaxis, the patient must be taught to keep the arms as close to the body as possible for any activity in which they are under a load. In this way, the effective lever arms remain short and the intra-articular pressure can be kept low. In really bad cases, shoulder pain can make contracture prophylaxis completely impossible. Analysis of the pain will show whether it is due to tenosynovitis, which can be treated by injections in the tendon, or arthritis in the humeroscapular joint or possibly in the acromioclavicular joint, which can be treated with intra-articular administration of steroids.

Dynamic muscle training is usually contraindicated, but occasionally it is necessary to train the muscles which lower the shoulders, as well as the triceps brachii, in preparation for walking with some form of support. With inflammation of the long biceps tendon, activation of the agonist (triceps muscle) can help to relax it. This so-called reciprocal innervation using the PNF technique can be used in many a painful condition (Knott 1964).

The elbow
(For anatomy and function, see p.39.)

Contracture prophylaxis in the elbow should also be carried out in a relaxed no-load condition and be as free from pain as possible. One should carry out the maximum movement in flexion, extension, pronation and supination. Any significant pain would make it impossible to carry through the contracture prophylaxis programme.

The pain could come from synovitides in the humero-ulnar or humeroradial joints. They can usually be treated by means of intra-articular steroid injections, administered laterally. Pain from the ulnar nerve and a weakness of the intrinsic muscles of the hand are signs that the nerve is hemmed in by proliferating synovial tissue. Lengthy compression can damage the nerve. With such symptoms, one must consider whether synovectomy on both the medial and lateral sides of the joint is called for, possibly with resection of the radial head. Intervention of this sort usually reduces the pain and at the same time helps to improve mobility (Brattström and Khudairy 1975).

The proximal radio-ulnar joint communicates with the elbow joint. The head of the radius can easily become damaged, with loss of supination and extension in the elbow joint.

Heavy exercising of the elbow muscles must be avoided, since any load on the elbow joint can lead to very considerable pressure being exerted on the joint, as explained earlier.

The wrist
(For anatomy and function, see p.42.)

Restriction of the movement of the wrist is usually less of a hindrance to the patient in everyday life, though flexion, extension and rotation of the wrist are required in a number of hobbies (for example, playing the piano or guitar, handicrafts, painting and various types of sport). Weakness and pain caused by radiocarpal and/or intercarpal synovitides or by tenosynovitides, particularly in the flexor tendons, can, on the other hand, have a very serious effect on general functional capacity. Pain always means weakness.

Treatment of the pain consists here too of steroid injections in the wrist, in the inflamed tendon sheaths or at their attachment points, as described earlier. Fixing the wrist using a wrist orthosis (see 'Orthoses', p.99) is also a possibility. If these treatments fail to eliminate the pain, and if X-rays show signs of progressive disease with a tendency to erosion, then synovectomy of the wrist may be necessary. Usually, the distal end of the ulna is resected at the same time. The prime purpose of the treatment is therefore to secure freedom from pain, rather than freedom of movement. Powerful exercise of the wrist is not usually necessary. However, there are theoretical reasons why innervation training of the extensor carpi ulnaris muscle can be of some assistance in alleviating the radial deviation of the metacarpus and thus in preventing ulnar deviation of the fingers (Andrén and Nordenskiöld 1976).

The hand
(For anatomy and function, see p.45.)

In order to maintain the function of the hand, it is essential that the patient should carry out a regular programme of contracture prophylaxis with the utmost care. In order to prepare for the exercises, the hands are first loosened up by immersing them for a while in hot water. If there are highly active synovitides, this should not be done, and a local application of steroid cream should be used instead. In the first phase of the exercises, the wrist is stabilised on the edge of a table, and first the distal interphalangeal joints, and then the bottom joints of the fingers are flexed. The interphalangeal joints should also be flexible when the bottom joints are extended. Myositides in the intrinsic muscles which have healed and been followed by fibrosis and shortening (intrinsic contracture) prevent these movements. Wherever possible, they should be carried out actively. If movement is prevented by contracture of the flexor tendons, then the movement could be assisted with the other hand.

In the second phase of the exercise, the fingers are fixed in a position of 5° ulnar deviation on the table and each finger in turn is moved over towards the thumb. This radial movement activates the intrinsic muscles. Opening the grip can be practised and tested using a tin of 8–10 cm diameter, which corresponds to normal requirements. Another important exercise for the hand function is flexion of the distal phalanx of the thumb. The IP joint can be exercised by maximum flexion, at the same time fixing the bottom joint with the thumb of the other hand.

Pain can hinder these exercises in all manner of ways and lead to inactivation from time to time. Bones and other structures which normally glide over one another suddenly experience increased friction. This reduces the mobility in the joints and tendons. The pain is largely caused by synovitides in the MCP and PIP joints, but can also be caused by tenosynovitides which can frequently occur on the volar side, in the carpal tunnel, and trap the median nerve (see 'The hand' p.45). The pain can be reduced by steroid injections, or in many cases by volar tenosynovectomy. Synovectomy is frequently indicated with the metacarpal joints II and III, which hold a key position in the function of the hand. Tenosynovitides along the flexor tendons can be treated with steroid injections repeatedly, but if they start to cause restriction of movement, and the risk of deformity becomes too great, then they should be surgically treated at once (Millender and Nalebuff 1975a, Helal 1984).

Any treatment of the hand and finger joints is primarily intended to prevent restriction of movement. Once deformity has set in, the joints become stressed in quite a different way and the risk of further damage and deformity elsewhere increases. Continual monitoring by qualified personnel enables any changes to be recognised at an early stage, so that optimal treatment can be given and surgical intervention carried out in good time. Heavy exercise of the finger flexors is contraindicated, but exercise of the extensors of the hand and fingers, which can easily become too long relatively speaking, is important.

Summary:

Contracture prophylaxis in the region of the upper extremities

- Exercises should be as relaxed as possible.

- Should wherever possible be carried out in a warm water pool.

- Should not give rise to any pain.

- Instruction should be given by a physiotherapist or ergotherapist who should also continually monitor mobility and function.

- Should include training of the radially innervated muscles.

- Total exclusion of exercises to strengthen finger flexors.

Adjusting the patient's way of life
(See also illustrated section, p.147.)
An analysis of the way the patient manages to cope with the requirements of everyday living forms the starting point for any programme of instruction on the protection of joints. The programme will be drawn up to fit the present needs of the situation and the demands made on the patient, including any arising out of their occupation (see also 'Day-to-day activities', p.79). If the stresses are too great for the protective mechanisms, there is a risk of damage to joint capsules and tendons, particularly if the muscles are already weakened or the joints are being incorrectly used, i.e. if the direction in which a joint is being loaded deviates considerably from the normal movement of that joint.

Joint protection in everyday situations means above all that in no situation whatsoever should a joint be subjected to a maximum load or stress. The patient must learn where the limits are and how best to space out individual activities, with rests in between. The following guidelines form the principal fundamentals of our joint protection programme (Cordery 1962, 1965, Chamberlain 1984).

Pain should be respected as a warning signal

Stiffness and pain on movement increase at times when the disease is active. Effective treatment is called for, either on a general basis or in the form of local anti-inflammatory measures. If pain occurs during the daily contracture prophylaxis exercises and if this persists for any time, one should take this as a sign that the joint has been overstressed and take appropriate measures to counter this situation.

As much movement as possible at home and at work

The patient should be encouraged to integrate all the everyday movements into the contracture prophylaxis programme: even washing up in warm water can serve as exercise. Many rheumatic patients find washing up quite pleasant, but the crockery must be light. Washing up machines are generally superfluous in such a household. However, the daily chores should never be seen as a substitute for the daily exercises.

Avoid, or cut to a minimum, anything which could cause deformity through 'internal' stress

From what we have previously said about the negative effects of the long flexor tendons on the stability of the MCP joints, it hardly needs to be said that any strong grip should be avoided. Jobs, such as stirring, wringing out, cutting, writing, sewing, etc. must be simplified and made easier. The use of any support for walking, which must obviously be firmly gripped if it is to be of any use at all, must always be preceded by a careful analysis of the load-bearing capacity of the upper extremities (see 'Walking Aids', p.110).

Avoid everything which could lead to deformity through 'external' stress

As well as internal stress, which arises out of the compressive forces of the muscles and traction from the tendons, one should pay particular attention to situations in which additional 'external' stress can give rise to deformity, for example, where a patient supports himself on a clenched fist or bent fingers when getting up. Another example of this would be where a patient holds a cup, a saucer, a pot or a tray with the fingers alone. Loading of this sort leads to ulnar deviation through overstressing the flexor tendons, and also to subluxation of the MCP joints. Other activities which are potentially damaging are undoing screw-type lids on jars, screw caps on bottles, turning keys or operating stiff knobs and handles. Here again, there is ulnar loading on the fingers, with an increasing risk of deformities developing. Other types of handle, for example on a refrigerator or car doors, can increase the risk of deformities of the thumb. Finally, we should mention that supporting one's head in one's hands or holding a book with extended PIP joints and angled MCP joints when reading lying down can cause ulnar deviation and swan neck deformities by shortening the intrinsic muscles.

Avoid one-sided, badly coordinated load situations of long duration
Extension of the muscles for a long period of time reduces the supporting effect of the joints themselves, so that the load is largely borne by the capsule and the ligaments. As a result, the ligaments become stretched, and instability and finally deformity occur. Any instability amounts to a new biomechanical situation for the joint. An example of such uneconomical use of one's physical resources would be carrying a heavy case for a long distance. False pride of this sort can end with ruptured tendons.

Distribute loads over a number of joint systems – shorten effective lever arms
Often, out of pure force of habit, patients will use only their fingers for certain tasks, such as lifting a coffee pot or a pan. The load could be spread over several joints if the other hand were used as well, as an additional support. The weight of a tray should be spread over the hand and forearm. Best of all would be to use a serving trolley of the correct height, thus avoiding any load whatsoever.

Wear only light clothing which is easy to put on
Dressing and undressing can give rise to unnecessary stress and avoidable pain in the joints involved in the operation. In principle, making special clothes for rheumatic patients does not present any particular problems. Clothes with adhesive fastenings and button strips at the front are recommended.

Cut out all superfluous activities
Occasionally, differences of opinion will arise with patients when one tries to reduce working loads. This requires great tact, and one must respect the patient's personality and wishes. Many jobs can be made much easier by using machines, or even cut out altogether.

Washing
A washing machine is of benefit to all but particularly for the rheumatic patient. It should be easy to open and close, but it may require a special gadget to enable the patient to operate the door mechanism. Normal washing machines will take about 3.5 kg of dry laundry, which corresponds to about 5 kg after spinning. Taking it out of the machine and hanging it up can put a considerable strain on

the shoulders and hands. Drying machines and cupboards are a great improvement; another member of the household could take care of hanging up wet clothes to dry.

Ironing
Ironing can lead to quite considerable strain on the shoulders, elbows, hand and finger joints, and can often cause pain. Clothing which requires no ironing has been a godsend. However, there are irons which are very light and do not cause strain on the joints.

Kitchen equipment
Preparing food involves a great deal of stress on the hands and arms. Much of the effort can be taken out of it by using machines, such as for kneading pastry and mincing meat, or peeling potatoes. Before such equipment is purchased, however, one should discuss with the patient what she used to do before the disease set in, and what she will have to do now. At all costs, one should avoid buying highly sophisticated equipment for which work can always be found, and leaving the patient with a guilty conscience for not making full use of it.

Housework
A good vacuum cleaner is essential if the rheumatic patient is to be able to keep the house clean herself. However, it is also important to plan the operation thoroughly in advance and carry it out in easy stages, and not to try and clean a 4-bedroom house in a morning, as one might have done in better times. A wrist orthosis can give valuable additional support. As a rule, the patient should avoid wringing out cloths, scrubbing and cleaning windows.

Seek the right balance of physical activity and rest
It is difficult, but extremely important to estimate correctly one's own capabilities where work is concerned. Patients must learn to gear their work load to their own physical abilities rather than to the expectations of others, and to assign top priority to establishing a rhythm in their work, while keeping a certain amount in reserve for other activities (see also 'Relaxation', p.132, also p.218, 224 and 225).

Summary:

Changes in life style and habits of working

- Respect pain.

- Move positively.
- Avoid 'external' stress.
- Avoid 'internal' stress.
- Avoid uncoordinated loads or stresses.
- Spread every load in time.
- Carefully select your tasks.
- Find your own balance between activity and rest pauses.

Technical aids (*see also illustrated section.*)
Technical aids were at one time often made by the patients themselves or by people close to them who were familiar with the problems. The results of these amateurish efforts were frequently makeshift arrangements of astonishing ugliness. No doubt this was often the reason why the handicapped frequently preferred to struggle on in their own way, rather than resort to technical aids which merely made them feel more inadequate than they actually were (Lannefelt, 1969, Roos *et al.* 1976). The development of modern aids, involving both designers and technicians, has done something to redress the balance and change attitudes; nowadays more trouble is taken to design aids which are attractive and acceptable to the handicapped and the healthy alike.

Light tools for specific purposes

Knife
To cut up a tomato or a piece of meat with a knife can cause the arthritis sufferer great pain if the MCP joints are inflamed and unstable. Cutting bread can also present problems as the knife has to be held firmly and the fingers bent in the ulnar direction. The patient often has insufficient strength to cut bread and meat. The Swedish Institute for the Handicapped, working closely with a group of designers (Ergonomi Design, Benktzon and Juhlin 1978) has developed a knife that meets the requirements of a patient with weak and painful wrists. The handle measures 23 × 34 mm in cross section and is set at an angle of 60° to the serrated blade. The knife is very light, well balanced and enables most patients to cut bread.

Gripping normal cutlery or holding a wine glass with a foot can also be a problem for the rheumatic patient. The same group of designers has therefore developed spoons, forks, a folding knife and a suitably shaped beaker in plexiglass. The cutlery has a good-sized telescopic handle and, like the beaker, is easy to hold (Benktzon and Juhlin 1978, 1984).

Large soft handles
Even though it may be unnecessary to redesign a tool for a particular job, it may still be helpful to bind or wrap the handles to enlarge them. Soft foam rubber, used for insulating pipes and all manner of other purposes nowadays, is very suitable for such applications and can easily be applied to cleaning brushes, the handles of pots and pans, mixing spoons, tooth brushes, garden tools etc. Walking aids can also be padded with foam rubber, but a leather covering on top is preferable, because of the high rate of wear and tear.

Reduce the effort required by using a longer lever arm
Many rotary movements present the arthritis sufferer with considerable problems. Turning on a normal tap with a conventional top applies considerable stress to the fingers, forcing them into ulnar deviation, and requiring a considerable amount of strength. Windows and balcony doors are also frequently difficult to open. A device which fits over the knob of the tap and has a long handle means that more leverage can be applied, and correspondingly less force is required. In fact, the principle of leverage can be used by the rheumatic patient in any situation where knobs and handles are small, not easily accessible, or difficult to operate, for example, most keys, the gas switches on a gas stove, window catches, the catches on a wheelchair, etc. Sorting out the details which cause the patient so much trouble in everyday life involves the therapist calling to take a closer look. It is then not too difficult for an orthopaedic workshop to design something with the patient and the therapist that will eliminate, or alleviate the problem. A universal grip has been designed which solves a lot of problems (see p.177).

Summary:

Technical aids

- Special technical aids which even healthy people will find attractive.

- Thick, soft grips and handles.

- Long lever arms.

Orthoses

Hand orthoses
(Swezey 1978, Ellis 1984, Simon *et al.* 1982.)
A hand orthosis can either serve a purely static, stabilising purpose or, where the wrist is fixed, can permit the fingers a certain amount of movement in face of a certain resistance, i.e. a dynamic effect. The effects of orthoses are a matter of discussion rather than fact as yet, and scientific investigation of their effectiveness in the case of deformities of the hand is still rare. It is, however, probable that certain types of orthosis, used in parallel with the other forms of treatment available, can alleviate pain, and can also be effective as a means of preventing, but not correcting, certain deformities.

Indications for static orthoses

Pain

Wrist pain caused by synovitides in the radiocarpal joints can often be helped by fixing the hand by means of a wrist orthosis (**31** and **32**). Such sleeves can be made of leather where they are likely to be subject to a great deal of wear and tear, or in softer plastic for less heavy duty. Simple casts or Kramer wire splints can be used at night, softly padded and attached to the hand with elastic strapping.

A wrist orthosis should hold the hand firmly in a position of $0-5°$ ulnar deviation and in slight extension. The thumb movement and the mobility of the bottom joints in a dorsovolar direction should not be restricted. It is also important to leave tactile areas of the hand uncovered, as far as possible. An orthosis that is too long could contribute to a stiffening of the proximal joints and restrict the flexion of the fingers.

Orthoses are best secured with Velcro in a way that will act against deformity, i.e. the strapping should support the metacarpus and the forearm in a volar direction.

If the measures described above are not successful in eliminating wrist pain within a period of a few months, one should then consider the possibility of a synovectomy of the wrist with simultaneous resection of the head of the ulna. If the pain in the MCP and PIP joints is severe, then a somewhat longer volar orthosis may be indicated for wearing at night, stabilising the fingers as well in a slightly flexed position. However, when using such splints, there is always a danger of restricting the movement of the finger joints, so that other forms of treatment such as local steroids, or even corrective surgery, should be considered as alternative or additional measures.

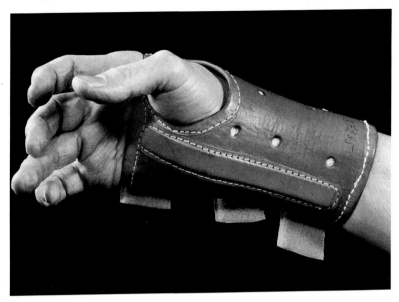

31 Static wrist orthosis in leather.

Indications for dynamic orthoses

Ulnar deviation

Ulnar deviation cannot be cured with dynamic orthoses. Deformities of the joints and pronounced weakness caused by marked ulnar deviation and dislocated tendons can, however, be slightly reduced by a dynamic orthosis with radial traction. The traction tape is wound round the fingers and holds the roots of the fingers. The dorsoradial force exerted acts in the opposite direction to the deformity and can strengthen the grip by correcting the axis of movement. The wrist is fixed. A carefully designed and fitted dynamic orthosis could in all probability maintain the mobility of the fingers and prevent contractures, which is also an important consideration before undertaking any joint surgery. There are various standard designs available (**33**). All of them are limited in scope, require very careful instruction of the patient, and should be checked frequently (Swanson 1984).

Thumb and PIP joint deformities

The three-point system can be used prophylactically against buttonhole deformities in the PIP joints. In this system, two pressure points act on the volar side, proximal and distal to the joint, and a third

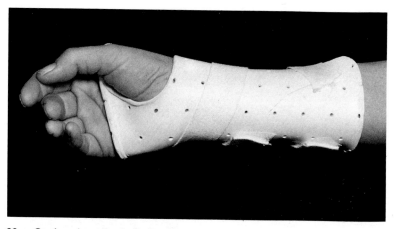

32a   Static wrist splint in Orthoplast.

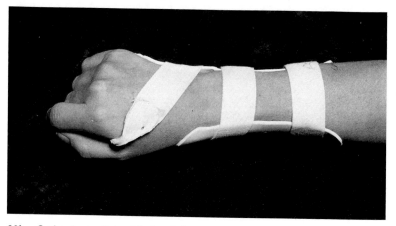

32b   Orthoplast splint, with thumb free.

pressure point is over the joint itself. With swan neck deformity, the same orthoses can be used in the initial stages – that is, if one decides in favour of an orthosis at all. The cuff is then turned, so that two pressure points are applied dorsally and one under the joint, in a central volar position.

It is also possible to use this system to counter the development of an extrinsic minus thumb flexion contracture in the MCP joint and hyperextension in the IP joint. The proximal pressure point in the three-point splint is attached to the wrist, while the distal one lies over the basal phalanx, and the middle one is placed over the basal joint to

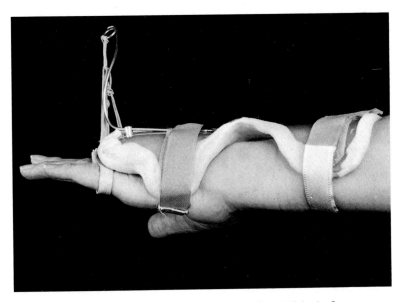

33 Corrective dorsal and lateral orthosis against ulnar drift in the fingers.

correct the flexion contracture. The orthoses described will have scarcely any corrective effect on existing deformities, though they will serve to remind the patient to carry out the contracture prophylaxis diligently.

Postoperative treatment by means of orthosis
After hand surgery, e.g. orthoplasty on the wrist joint, orthoses designed to reinforce the aim of the operation and the postoperative training, may be necessary. In most cases, orthoses with radial traction provided by rubber bands and appropriate support are used for such purposes. The most important preparatory work is that of the ergotherapist, while the final fitting is the responsibility of the surgeon. In this way, flexion training of the PIP joints can be achieved by fixing the MCP joints in extension.

All orthoses should be comfortable for the patient to wear and it should be possible to put them on and take them off again without any difficulty. A well-used orthosis is a sure sign of an orthosis which fits well and reduces pain. In recent times, Orthoplast and Plastazote have been used a great deal, and are easy to mould. They can also be re-fitted. Polyform is usually too stiff. Any orthosis treatment of the hands should run in conjunction with a carefully organised programme of contracture prophylaxis and constant monitoring by the therapist. The patient should understand the purpose of the orthosis treatment and know how long to wear it each day.

Summary:

Orthoses for the upper extremities

- Static orthoses, especially with pain.

- Dynamic orthoses to maintain mobility and correct axis of movement.

- Special postoperative orthoses.

- Orthoses should be pleasant to wear.

- Careful instruction and checking of patient.

Back and lower extremities

Contracture prophylaxis

Hip, knee, foot and toe joints

> Motto: It is always easier to prevent deformities than to cure them

The patient and his family should always be well informed about the planning of the programme of contracture prophylaxis. Exercises for load-bearing joints are best carried out with the patient in a relaxed state in a warm water pool, but could also be carried out with the patient lying on a firm surface covered with foam rubber. Where traction is given in the home (e.g. for contracture of the knee), special equipment is available (Persson 1975). The lower extremities should always be considered as a single functional unit in contracture prophylaxis. The programme is drawn up to reflect the patient's daily schedule, his day-to-day activity status and the stresses occasioned when sitting, standing and walking.

The mobility of the hips is examined with the patient lying down. The opposite hip and knee joints are kept in a position of maximum flexion in order to prevent the lumbar lordosis. The patient will notice at once whether there is any contracture because the affected leg will lift off the surface on which the patient is lying.

Knee mobility: flexion and extension are also checked with the patient lying on a firm flat surface. The patient can check whether he is able to press the leg down on to the surface or whether this is prevented by a loss of extension. These exercises are carried out for each side separately.

The heels can be examined with the patient lying down or standing, if the patient bends slightly forwards and supports himself against a wall with his arms. Mobility of the toes, particularly extension of the big toe, is best examined in conjunction with a cream massage after washing the feet.

Pain in the hip and knee joints can make it very difficult to carry out a carefully planned programme of contracture prophylaxis, or even make it impossible altogether. The pain is generally caused by synovitides in the joints, or tenosynovitides in the region of the tendon insertions. In the hip region, it is the gluteus medius tendon and the bursae of the trochanter major, as well as the proximal adductor tendons, that are affected, while in the knee, it is the insertions of the tendons on the tibia medial above the pes anserinus and also laterally on the fibula, and possibly also the connective tissue in the proximal tibiofibular joint. The treatment of pain consists in particular of local steroid injections, after careful examination of the actual causes. Long drawn out processes, with the risk of deformities occurring, should be examined and assessed by the orthopaedic specialist, who may have to carry out a synovectomy or tenotomy.

Foot hygiene

Foot hygiene is an important matter for the rheumatic patient. Frequently, painful pressure sores occur on arthritic feet above the sharp edges of the inner bones, particularly if the patient is not wearing suitable shoes (too small or too narrow). These wounds can quickly become infected, and the infection can affect the patient's general wellbeing, apart from making it very difficult to walk. A single painful toe can have a surprisingly restricting effect on a patient's ability to walk. Nowadays, patients with chronic polyarthritis are fitted with prostheses in hips, and knees, and sometimes also in ankle joints. With such surgery it is important, both before the operation and afterwards, to keep any source of infection under control and to give appropriate treatment.

Summary:

Contracture prophylaxis

- In as relaxed a state as possible.
- Best of all in a warm water pool.

- On a flat, relatively firm surface.
- Should be carried out without pain.
- Careful foot hygiene as prophylaxis against infections.

Rest positions and lying down (*see also illustrated section*)
Although it is not possible to lay down hard and fast rules about the type of bed to be used, there are a number of fundamentals that could usefully be explained. In order to make it easier for the patient to get into and out of bed, the bed itself should be approximately 40–50 cm high. A 10–15 cm thick polyester mattress should be used, on a firm base, even though many patients would prefer something softer. In any event, the mattress should not mould itself too closely to the shape of the body because the bed would then be unsuitable for carrying out the programme of contracture prophylaxis exercises, and there would be the risk of overlooking a contracture in the early stages. Where there are obvious flexion contractures in the hip joint, suitable bolsters can be used to prevent compensating contractures in the knee. If contracture already exists in the knees, compensating hip contractures can be avoided by means of a so-called terrace bed. Both types of treatment can be found in clinics in particular, where patients with a high risk of contracture can be treated and observed.

Cushions under the knees are not permitted. Painful synovitides in the knee are better treated with intra-articular steroid injections or with chemical, radiological or surgical synovectomy. Cushions between the knees can prevent adduction contracture. A firm cushion or pillow or an adjustable board set up for the feet can prevent dangerous plantar flexion of the feet. A tunnel which protects the feet from the weight of the bedclothes, is also recommended.

Patients with a tendency to contracture in the hips and knees should lie flat on their stomachs once or twice a day for half an hour and let their feet hang down over the end of the bed. Contractures in the hips and knees are frequently found in juvenile chronic polyarthritis and in ankylosing spondylitis. Some patients are very unwilling to lie on their stomachs, others get used to it in time but need help to turn over again. In any case, the condition of the patient's shoulders and neck plays a very important part. If it is not possible for them to lie on their stomachs, then they can lie on their back on a flat bed, with a small cushion under the knees for the time being to compensate for the lordosis of the lumbar spine.

Sitting position (*See also 'Chairs', p.107.*)

Consciously sitting in the correct position is an important factor in the prophylaxis of conditions involving the back and the lower extremities. Chairs should have higher seats than usual, in order to keep the stress on the knee joints as low as possible when the patient stands up again, and the back should be well supported from the level of the 3rd lumbar vertebra. The length of the seat should also be adapted to the length of the thigh, while the back should be inclined at an angle of 110° to the rear.

Working tables should correspond in height to the chair they are used with. If the table top is too high, then the arms will get tired too quickly, while if it is too low, it could induce unphysiological kyphosis of the neck and back.

Many sufferers who work in an office must be able to reach their typewriter, dictating machine, telephone and desk drawers. A swivel chair can help prevent unnecessary strain on the knees and back in such cases. In order to spare the neck, the telephone should be set at an appropriate height, and if the hand and finger joints are affected, there are suitable models available nowadays with pushbutton dialling. Electric typewriters are much easier on the hands.

The car is nowadays the most important means of transport. Ankylosing spondylitis patients in particular often have considerable difficulty in driving. One can try to adapt the seat to the patient's individual needs with cushions and backrests. If a hip condition means that the patient must sit at an angle, then one should try to counter this with aids of one sort or another so that the patient is sitting with the hips symmetrically balanced. In juvenile chronic polyarthritis and pelvic spondylitis, an incorrect sitting position can easily lead to scoliosis. Extra mirrors compensate for stiffness in the neck.

Severe conditions of the hips or knees can in certain circumstances be compensated for by using a chair with a divided seat, or one in which the seat is soft and yielding on one side.

Changes in life style

The same rules apply to conditions of the lower extremities as to those of the upper extremities:

Respect pain

Pain always indicates that a joint is overstressed. The reason for the pain should always be evaluated. A painful joint is always kept in the position in which the pain is at its lowest. Stiffening in this position usually indicates a functional hindrance. In ankylosing spondylitis, pain and contracture can occur in the region of the cervical spine. Owing to the high risk of contracture, treatment of the pain and physiotherapy are of paramount importance.

Pain is a sign that the disease is active. Generally speaking, anti-inflammatory drugs are used during this stage. Local treatment is aimed at reducing stress on the joints and keeping the limbs in the most favourable position, and local corticosteroid infiltrations are used.

Keep on the move in your everyday life
When working, a frequent change of position is recommended. Frequent changes from standing to sitting and vice versa are also advisable.

Avoid rest positions which could promote deformities, such as chairs that are too low, or beds that are too soft!

Take care to stress the joints in the functionally and anatomically correct way and avoid any rotational stress!
Contractures always lead to changes in biomechanical conditions. Unstable and deformed joints are at greater risk from incorrect movements than those in the correct functional position.

Always distribute the load (see 'Walking aids', p.110.)

Avoid one-sided or badly coordinated loads of any duration

Find your own balance between activity and rest. (See also illustrated section at the end of the book.)

Technical aids *(see also illustrated section)*

Chairs
A patient who has difficulty in walking but has to do the housework will need a suitable chair for working. The most popular chairs are those with individually adjustable seats, which can also be adjusted for height, which is very important. Upholstered, adjustable and detachable arm rests and individually adapted back rests are also further advantages. The cloth covering should be of corduroy or some other suitable cloth with a high degree of friction. The chair should run on wheels which can be braked, while the brake levers should be long, easy to reach and easy to operate. Some people are inclined to see

wheels as a possible source of accidents. However, it has been found in practice that even people with the severest of handicaps, who are practically confined to a wheelchair, prefer to use a chair on wheels when they are working, and even use it as a means of transport at home, pushing themselves off with their feet and frequently travelling backwards.

Patients who have difficulty sitting down, for example those with one or both knees stiff, will find a chair with a divided seat, the front part of which is individually adjustable, a considerable advantage. For patients with severe hip conditions, standing chairs or chairs with saddle-shaped seats or chairs designed from plaster casts of the patient's seat and hips, can bring enormous relief. If the knees are weak and unstable, a chair with a catapult seat could be an advantage. These chairs must be very carefully adjusted to the patient's weight, and they are primarily intended to be used for relaxation and are therefore not fitted with wheels. Modern varieties in which the seat is electrohydraulically controlled are the most practical as the patient is raised slowly.

Normal armchairs, possibly with raised legs, are suitable for relaxation or watching television. Individual companies manufacture furniture specially suited to the needs of the elderly and the handicapped. Anything temporary or makeshift is usually more of a hindrance than a help in everyday life, or when doing the housework. Spare cushions are useful when going out, or if additional seating is required at home. In the office or other place of work, where one must be able to move about freely, arm rests often restrict movement and should therefore be detachable. In most cases, 'rocking chair' footrests are a considerable help when seated.

More than a third of all patients suffering from chronic polyarthritis and the majority of those with ankylosing spondylitis have neck problems, often causing considerable pain on movement and restriction of movement. In such cases, a suitable support for the neck is essential. The working chair described above can be fitted with a neck support, and many types of arm chair have high backs and wings.

If a special chair has been prescribed for a patient as a technical aid, the physiotherapist or ergotherapist should instruct the patient fully on how to use it, especially how to sit and stand up. Standing up from a sitting position can place a considerable strain on the knees and wrists. However, using the correct technique, the patient will find it much easier. The patient places one foot slightly ahead of the other, shifts the weight of the top part of the body as far forward as possible and after rocking lightly to and fro to start with, finally stands up.

There is no need to support oneself with the hands. Instruction and practice will give the doctor or therapist an opportunity to have a further chat about contracture prophylaxis.

All these aids, including chairs and 'rocking chair' footrests, are only fully effective if the patient accepts them as an integral part of the medical and functional treatment, like physiotherapy, operations and medicaments, and uses them also at times when the disease is less active.

The bathroom

The extent to which the patient is able to cope with matters of hygiene unaided will usually depend on the size and layout of the bathroom, and how it is equipped (see also 'Adapting the home', p.123). Raised or specially built-up toilet seats are as a rule essential for patients with knee or hip contractures. Difficulties in getting up can be overcome by using the appropriate technique and with the aid of suitable rails on the walls, and possible detachable supports. A good firm stool is also required, so that one can undress sitting down. The bath itself should have a platform to sit on, and if necessary some form of lifting aid. Grab bars on the wall and non-slip mats are also important, though the latter will wear and require occasional replacement. A long-handled brush, light and with a suitably thick handle, will enable patients even with considerable restriction in the upper extremities, to wash themselves properly. All the taps should be of a kind the patient can comfortably operate, or be replaced by a single-handed mixer tap with thermostat as part of the process of adapting the home (see p.174).

Summary:

Chairs and bathroom equipment

- Surfaces of all seats including WC should be higher than normal.

- Work chairs on wheels.

- Easy chair with neck support.

- Footrests, rocking chair footrests.

- Platform in bath, grab bars, lift.

- Stool in bathroom.

- Careful instruction in all types of movement, e.g. sitting down and standing up, climbing into and out of the bath.

Walking aids (*see also illustrated section*)
Walking aids for arthritis patients should be light and designed in such a way that they are suited to the individual arm and hand functions of the patient. If their lower extremities are affected, arthritis patients must often resort to walking aids to ease the strain and spread the weight over all four extremities as it were. Part of the body weight is transferred to the upper extremities. The walking aid must therefore be selected so that the load on the upper extremities does not exceed the limit. The type of walking aid used will depend on the condition of the patient's hands and arms.

An essential requirement for the use of walking aids is mobility and strength in the fingers, freedom from pain and as near full extension in the elbow joint as possible. In this way, it will be possible to avoid any excessive intra-articular pressure and to guarantee relatively efficient relief of pain in the shoulders (Deaver 1966, Althoff 1973).

The walking stick
A walking stick is necessary if the strain on the lower extremities has to be reduced, while the upper extremities, and in particular the hands, can still take the weight. The handle should be well padded, so that the effort required to hold the stick firmly is reduced. A thin leather loop will help to hold the stick when not actually walking with it, e.g. when standing in shops, etc., or when the hand is required for something else, like opening a door.

The length of the stick should be such that when used for support, the elbow and wrist are extended (see p.205). With flexion contracture of the elbow, special measures would be required (see below). A light wooden stick weighs about 240 g. The use of a stick can be facilitated by means of broad handles with anatomically accurate moulding. In the case of severe deformities of the hand, a special handle can be designed from a cast of the hand and fastened to the handle of the stick (Brattström 1974). When lack of balance is the main problem the stick could be designed as a pilgrim staff.

The elbow crutch
Elbow crutches come in a variety of different shapes and sizes, some with angled and some with horizontal arm support. One model that can be recommended is the Kalmar crutch, which has a comfortable handle of wood and a velvet lining. The handle and arm support together form an angle of 110°, so that the wrist is loaded in a straight position. Crutches with handles that are too hard, or that are insufficiently angled, forcing the elbow forward, are unsuitable. The lightest models weigh about 550 g.

If the patient's hands are painful or deformed by contracture and his grip is much weakened, then the Althoff crutch (ca. 740 g) may be recommended. This has a grip that is relatively thick and can be adjusted in three places, so that the hand can be loaded in the most favourable position. However, the adjustment must be carried out very carefully. If the patient wears a wrist orthosis, on one or both wrists, this fact must be taken into consideration, and it may be necessary for one type of aid to be adapted to the other during manufacture.

Shoulder crutches

Shoulder crutches are needed if the strain on hands, fingers and elbows would be too great for the patient to bear using any other form of walking aid. However, taking the strain in the axilla makes considerable demands on the shoulders, and can increase the pain and destruction in those joints. In rare cases, branches of the plexus brachialis can be damaged by the additional strain. The shoulder joints can be partly protected from the strain by adequate padding, or the padded crutch can also be supported to an extent by the thorax. The handles must be carefully adapted to the hands. If the hands are badly deformed, then the handles should be shaped after a plaster cast, for even a hand with insufficient strength to grip can still hold a crutch steady. For especially severe cases, there are specially adapted walking aids, with or without wheels, which would require some measure of adaptation to the individual patient and his surroundings.

The walking stick or crutch should give the maximum support to the damaged side and is therefore carried on the other side. In this way, the effective torsion (the relieving force × distance from the axis of movement of the affected joint) is at its maximum (**24**). With multiple destructions or painful joints, one may be forced to compromise, i.e. to use the aid alternatively on the right or left side.

One should not forget that walking aids should have suitable rubber grommets or spikes to prevent slipping, depending on whether they are intended for indoor or outdoor use. It goes without saying that initial training in the use of the aid should be given, and that continual checks should be made on the fit of the handle and the way the aid is being used.

Summary:

Walking aids

• Analysis of the particular loading problem.

- Analysis of the function, load-bearing capacity and need for an orthosis in the region of the upper extremities.

- Selection and prescription of the most suitable walking aids.

- Careful fitting.

- Monitoring.

Orthoses
Knee orthosis
With painful and inflamed knees it is often necessary to provide additional support in the form of elastic bandages or strapping, reinforced at the side. Elastic knee caps with Heussner spring are particularly helpful. In other cases, bandages with adhesive fastenings (Velcro) can be recommended. Any form of lacing is not suitable for arthritis sufferers. Painful knees with a tendency to flexion contracture can be suitably stabilised with a Creutz splint. This consists of a leather-covered stay which is fixed to the back of the leg above and below the knee with broad straps. A padded plastic or plaster cast, designed for the maximum extension, will serve much the same purpose, if the shape is altered accordingly when the contracture begins to change.

Synovitides and impending contractures should also be treated with traction in the longitudinal direction of the lower leg. If a knee with a slight flexion contracture is fixed in the extended position without any further treatment, compression fractures can occur at the condyles of the femur, because the edge of the tibia, which has been dorsally luxated, exerts too much pressure (25). Any long-term confinement in a splint can lead to hypotrophy of the quadriceps. This gives rise to instability in the joint.

Knee bandages with hinges are as a rule too heavy for the rheumatic patient. Long leg splints, on the other hand, may provide good support when walking if the knees are unstable. In addition to the normal models with double metal struts, inner shoe, knee joint and special locking device, there are others with single-sided struts constructed on the three-point principle which require very careful fitting and are suitable for people of low body weight with a mild valgus position (Smith *et al.* 1970, Perry 1967).

Any type of splint involves the risk of a further restriction of mobility. One should also not overlook the fact that putting the splint on and taking it off again with deformed and rheumatic hands can be a very difficult undertaking. Progress in knee surgery has reached the stage nowadays that one generally tries to use an endoprosthesis in which the inner stabilisation makes an external orthosis superfluous. The majority of such operations are successful.

Heel orthoses
Painful ankles can make walking impossible, since these joints have to bear the entire weight of the body when walking. Bandages are usually of little use, although the figure-of-eight bandage can give some relief. Extended shoe supports or shoes with reinforcing stitching which prevent eversion and inversion movement in the ankle can also be helpful. However, quite often the problem is attributable to synovitides which affect both the talocrural joint and the subtalar joints and therefore call for complete immobilisation. Formerly, special leather 'jackets' with lacing were made for the purpose. These were very difficult for the patient to put on and also meant in most cases that special shoes were also required. Present-day models in leather or Orthoplast are light and still give the required degree of stability. However, special shoes are still needed with them. It is also important to point out to any orthopaedic workshop involved that rheumatic patients make fewer demands in respect of resistance to wear and loading, so that the aids produced are not unnecessarily heavy (and expensive).

Summary:

Orthoses

- Knee bandages, preferably light ones, with reinforcing on the medial and lateral sides, possibly with adhesive fastening.

- Heavy knee bandages for unstable knees are rarely satisfactory. In most cases, surgical replacement of the knee is to be preferred.

- Light ankle bandages may prove useful but special shoes are required.

Shoes as a means of joint protection in chronic polyarthritides
(Jan Pahle, Björn Grönli)

The sooner the rheumatic patient appreciates the importance of wearing the right kind of shoe, the better for the protection of his joints. Even a single painful toe can, in unfavourable circumstances, considerably affect his ability to walk or change his gait in such a way that the joints are unduly and improperly stressed. A rheumatic foot, especially one that is damaged and unstable in the forefoot, with hallux valgus, is broader than normal, and the damage to the metatarsophalangeal joints with dorsal luxation and hammer toes also changes the height of the foot by comparison with a healthy foot. Hyperkeratosis, gradually leading to open pressure sores, can form wherever a damaged joint immediately below the skin and subcutis is subjected to stress or pressure.

Where the talocrural and subtalar joints in particular have been affected, the foot is sensitive to pressure from the side, and must be supported by the shoe in the mid-position between eversion and inversion.

With children suffering from juvenile chronic polyarthritis, there is a stronger tendency to deformities than in adults, due to the

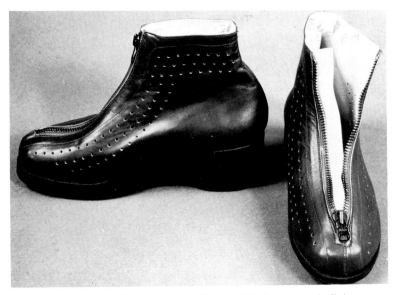

34 High-sided shoes for rheumatic sufferers, with zip fastener, built-in support and extremely well padded tongue. Available in 7 different widths.

continuing growth. The greatest care should therefore be exercised in the selection and subsequent monitoring of shoes. Although deformi-

35   Semi-open shoes for rheumatic sufferers with built-in support and long lacing but relatively thick laces. Available in 7 different widths.

36   Very light, airy open shoe with built-in support and Velcro adhesive fastening. Available in 7 different widths.

ties of the feet rarely allow the patient to wear ready made shoes, a good orthopaedic workshop can provide some individual styling in the more straightforward cases. Severe damage and deformity call for specially made shoes, starting from a print or cast. Nowadays, it is possible to make even orthopaedic shoes appear reasonably elegant, but all too often there are not enough skilled craftsmen, and time is usually pressing. For this reason, a number of standard models have been developed which can be obtained from special shops for the handicapped (**34–36**).

Shoe supports
These are inserts which are specially adapted to the foot, especially the longitudinal and transverse arches. Under the forefoot, for example, in a retrocapital position, there is a small support pad. Although such supports can be used nowadays in various types of shoes, it is advisable to make sure that they are compatible. The materials used in their making usually consist of metal plate, normally covered with leather for comfort. Nowadays, Plastazote is frequently used, since it can be shaped better to the foot and can also be covered with leather. Supports are designed to relieve pressure on sensitive parts of the foot and to spread it over areas which are less sensitive. They can also improve lateral stability and serve a prophylactic purpose with regard to varus and valgus deformities. In any case, such supports can protect the foot from the consequences of disease or alleviate them, provided stout shoes are worn. Soft slippers with supports are just plain ridiculous.

The right kind of shoe (see also **34–36***)*
Even healthy feet will suffer from bad shoes. This is as good a time as any to warn against wearing gym shoes, which are intended for use in sport, but are not designed for everyday wear. Shoes are intended to transfer the body weight to the ground and distribute it. They should fit snugly and be tightly laced up in order to keep the heel in the heel cap. The middle part of the shoe transfers the load from the heel to the forefoot. It should be particularly stout and above all, the longitudinal axis should not be capable of deformation. The sole of the forefoot should be soft but thick enough that any unevenness in the ground cannot be felt. It is also an advantage if there is room in the shoe to stretch the basal joints of the toes.

It is worth repeating here that the sole and the uppers should be cut in such a way that the foot has enough room in every direction. Above all, it is essential to ensure that the big toe is not pressed inwards, as often happens in badly fitting shoes in the course of the normal heel-to-toe action. Part of the body weight is transferred to the forefoot via the heel. At the same time, the heel serves as a brake when the foot touches the ground at the beginning of the standing phase. The best height for the heel is between 25 and 40 mm, as higher heels transfer too large a proportion of the body weight on to the damaged metatarsophalangeal joints. This effect is reinforced if the inner sole in the region of the heel does not take the form of a horizontal load surface. Too high and too pointed heels lead to instability in the heel, since the position of the joint is unfavourable and the lever arm is too long. If the foot has any tendency to a varus or valgus position, then it is necessary to raise the inside or outside wall of the heel. However, one can only expect this measure to be successful if the shoe is sufficiently high to keep the ankle stable.

We have already discussed adapting shoes when an orthosis is worn on the foot.

Shoe fastenings

Shoes fit best if they are tied with long laces or held on by a broad piece of elastic. The tongue should extend under the laces and reach up over the top of the shoe, to give adequate protection against anything that could apply pressure to the foot and damage it. Tying laces with rheumatic hands can be a problem. Elastic shoe laces can help, or an elastic wedge attached to the top of the uppers. Occasionally, zip fasteners which can be pulled up or down with the aid of a hook, provide the answer.

As rheumatic feet are often swollen, the lacing should be adaptable. With large variations, insoles could be used to compensate.

If the toes are very stiff, and if the foot cannot be rolled sufficiently in the normal way, the sole can be fitted with a special roll. A wedge-shaped rubber insert can be built into the heel. The latter is particularly useful with pain in the talonavicular and talocrural joint, or if the ankle is stiff from surgery. Recently, inserts have been introduced for the heel as well.

The question of materials

Leather is the chosen material. The rheumatic patient sweats heavily and most other materials are too impermeable to permit proper ventilation. Contact allergies can be avoided if one takes care not to buy shoes dyed in aniline dyes. It is important that the shoes should be light, particularly if there is a difference in the length of leg to compensate for. Lighter grades of leather are admittedly not so hard-wearing, but rheumatic people do far less walking than healthy people and therefore occasion much less wear. Soft insoles, for example of Plastazote, lose their shape after a while and should always be replaced in good time. Where the difference in length of leg to be accommodated is more than 1 cm, the heel and sole should be increased, and if the height of the heel cap is sufficiently great, a part of the difference can be compensated inside the shoe, which would be far less obvious.

Summary of points on shoes

- Stability in the longitudinal axis: it should not be possible to turn the shoe round its longitudinal axis, when it is held by the toe and heel.

- Firm heel caps which fit snugly.

- Lacing (fastening) must hold the foot stable in the heel cap.

- Broad forefoot section, plenty of space for the toes.

- Soft insoles, shaped to the foot if possible, best of all with support pad under the forefoot to relieve stress.

- Upright inner edge in forefoot section, so that the big toe is never restricted at any stage of the foot movement. A firm fit does not imply that the toes are pressed together.

- Sufficiently wide heel, between 25 and 40 mm high.

- Rubber and possibly additional buffer heel for better contact and additional shock absorption.

- Relatively thick soft forefoot sole.

- Compensation for leg length difference.

Wooden clogs
Opinions with regard to wooden clogs for arthritis patients are mixed. Some patients enjoy wearing them, above all at home. The usual models are quite high above the forefoot, but have no heel cap. On the whole, wooden shoes barely match up to the criteria set for good shoes. Nevertheless, putting them on and taking them off is simple, there is plenty of ventilation for the foot, and the forefoot is immobilised. Wooden clogs that fit, in our experience, can actually alleviate pain in diseased metatarsophalangeal joints. In spite of the absence of a heel cap, patients with none-too-serious changes to the ankle do actually have the feeling, both when standing and walking, that they are secure.

Summary:

- Foot problems affect the overall functional capacity of the rheumatic sufferer.

- Foot problems should be investigated by patient, orthopaedic surgeon, rheumatologist, technician and physiotherapist and possibly ergotherapist, all working together to find a solution.

- Pain-free feet which can take the weight are an invaluable protection for other joints.

The rheumatic patient confined to a wheelchair

In the initial stages of the disease, rheumatic patients see the wheelchair as a threatening spectre. Patients who have great difficulty in walking on account of disease in their hips and knees may struggle on for a long time before accepting the benefits that a wheelchair can undoubtedly bring. Even the doctor treating the patient may see the wheelchair as something of a failure, and consider that with it go the last vestiges of mobility.

The following investigation into the problem is based on a series of interviews and examinations carried out with 40 patients of the Rheumatism Outpatients Centre in Lund who were prescribed a wheelchair in the years 1969–1976 (Brattström *et al.* 1981), and on a study of rheumatic patients confined to wheelchairs in Central Sweden (Brattström *et al.* 1977).

Indications for a wheelchair

Indications for a wheelchair are severely restricted walking ability outside the home and the need for effective relief of stress and weight on the knee and/or hip joints. Social reasons, too, i.e. making social contact with the family, friends and acquaintances easier, and enabling the patient to attend social functions as well, may be decisive factors in prescribing a wheelchair. If numerous joints are generally attacked by the disease, rheumatic sufferers take to walking 'on all fours', i.e. they seek to take the weight off their hips, knees and ankles as much as they can by using a variety of supports and aids. The difficulties that lead to the wheelchair can therefore lie in both the lower and the upper extremities. Most frequently, however, it is the knees, often together with hip problems, which make walking impossible. More rarely, painful feet can prove such a problem that the patient requires a wheelchair.

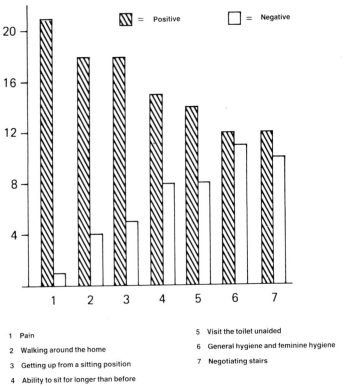

1 Pain	5 Visit the toilet unaided
2 Walking around the home	6 General hygiene and feminine hygiene
3 Getting up from a sitting position	7 Negotiating stairs
4 Ability to sit for longer than before	

37 Results of hip and knee joint replacement operations with reference to seven different functions among 25 patients at the polyclinic in Lund.

Scope of the wheelchair

Wheelchairs are almost exclusively provided for transport outside the home. In the home, the rheumatic patient should use the wheelchair only in extreme situations. Nowadays, surgical intervention in the form of hip and knee joint replacements should make it possible for every patient to retain a minimum walking capacity (**37**).

The home (see also 'Adapting the home', p.123.)

The patient confined to a wheelchair needs his surroundings to be free from stairs, door sills, narrow passages and corridors. The kitchen should be organised and equipped so that work can be carried out sitting down, while in the bathroom there should be sufficient room to bring the wheelchair right up to the WC. There should also be plenty of space to store or park the wheelchair in or near the home. It is not only the motorist who has parking problems.

120

Table 1   Technical aids of 40 wheelchair patients at the Polyclinic in Lund

	Helps	Doesn't help	Not received
Working chair on wheels	23	8	4
Coxarthrosis chair	5	3	1
Catapult seat	9	15	0
Special seat cushions	32	2	1
Reading desk	19	3	4
Rocking chair type foot rest	15	6	1
Raised WC	34	4	0
Closomat	6	0	0
Electric bed	9	1	4

M. Brattström et al. 1981.

Technical aids

There are a number of technical aids which can make life easier for the severely handicapped patient who has difficulty in walking. First of all, there is the working chair on wheels with a long brake handle, special chair seats, raised toilet seats, reading tables and even rocking chair type foot rests (Table 1). In exceptional cases, a catapult chair may be needed to raise the patient, by means of a powerful spring, from a sitting position. As stated before, a chair of this sort requires special adjustment and checking.

The Closomat is a special type of WC with adjustable automatic flushing and warm air drying. A toilet of this sort is a godsend for the patient with severely restricted arm and hand function or a tendency to perianal eczema. Beds with electrical adjustment of the head and foot of the bed and height adjustment help the disabled to raise themselves up from a lying to a sitting position and to transfer from the bed to the wheelchair unaided. Many patients need a wheelchair to get into and out of the car.

The patient needs to be thoroughly and carefully instructed in the proper use of technical aids and must practise using them. The possibility of deterioration in functional capacity makes it necessary to have continuous checking and frequent readjustments to new situations. Most of the technical aids given to the patients were used.

Contracture prophylaxis

A patient confined to a chair or wheelchair, who has come to appreciate the danger of contracture during the course of his illness, will appreciate the significance of a regular programme of contracture

Table 2   Does the wheelchair come at the right time?

	Functional capacity			
	II	III	IV	
Yes	1	6	15	=22
No – patient could have used it earlier	1	6	11	=18

40 patients

M. Brattström *et al.* 1981.

prophylaxis. If he is properly instructed, he will accept the measures prescribed. Lying outstretched on a flat bed is an important exercise and should be repeated several times a day for approximately half an hour. The correct design for a wheelchair individually adapted to the needs of the patient and its proper use are also a part of the contracture prophylaxis. Even if the wheelchair is only used outside the home, it should be equipped with folding foot rests. As the hands can only rarely be used for propelling the chair with chronic polyarthritis patients, models with large wheels on the rear axles are recommended.

In the home, patients with severely restricted function in the knees and hips should use a working chair fitted with wheels, in which they can push themselves off with their feet, which would have the effect of stimulating the quadriceps muscles. On the other hand, if the wheelchair is needed in the home as well, then one should at all costs attempt to retain at least some small measure of independence, for example, in transferring from one seat to another, to the bed, or to the WC. These vestiges of independence and some small capacity for walking which have been saved by the surgeon and physiotherapist leave the patient with a shimmer of hope and optimism in the majority of cases. The chair is then seen as a technical aid like any other, representing only a small part of the overall rehabilitation process, along with medical, surgical and other measures. After having accepted the wheelchair 18 of 40 patients admitted that they had needed it earlier (Table 2).

Electric wheelchairs can bring a great deal of pleasure into the patient's life in summer in the appropriate surroundings, but in general their scope is limited. They can be used in the home only in special situations, if there is plenty of room to move about, with lifts large enough to take them and ready access to the outside, or in hospitals or other large buildings with long corridors. In more restricted circumstances, such a chair is more likely to have an immobilising effect than to enrich the patient's daily life.

If the patient wishes to have an electric wheelchair for use outside the house, then one should take the following into consideration:

- The wheelchair must be tried out and adapted to the patient's needs.

- The patient must be thoroughly instructed in the use of the wheelchair in his own surroundings.

- There must be a parking space for the chair in the immediate vicinity of the home.

- Prompt and reliable servicing facilities must be available.

- Electric wheelchairs should usually not be used in the home.

Summary:

- The wheelchair serves to take the weight and stress off the joints of the lower and upper extremities, in particular the hips, knees, hands and shoulders.

- The wheelchair must be adapted to meet individual requirements: foot rest, large wheels on the rear axle, neck support, long brake lever, special seat cushion.

- The home must also be adapted for the wheelchair.

- Proper equipment with other technical aids.

- Continuing contracture prophylaxis.

- Wheelchair only used in the home in special circumstances.

- Electric wheelchair also in special circumstances, especially in clinics.

- Instruction, constant supervision and any necessary additional or supplementary aids.

Adapting the home

Arthritis sufferers with reduced functional capacity are dependent on their practical surroundings, suitably adapted to their particular disability. This applies not only to the home but also to their place of work and to any leisure activities they may enjoy. One of the aims is to keep the strain on their joints to a minimum. It is therefore often necessary to make corresponding changes in their surroundings. It goes without saying that this must be preceded by careful thought, analysis and planning. The following measures will be required:

- Home visit when one can meet the family and discuss with them. As a rule, such visits can provide a great deal of vital information.
- Analysis and assessment of the functions the patient is still capable of.
- Contact with the local authorities for planning purposes.
- Continuous monitoring of the situation after completion of the changes.

The patient should afterwards be able to do the following:

- to move about unaided, go out and come back in again,
- to cook,
- to eat,
- to clean, wash and look after his or her clothes,
- to sleep and to make love,
- to keep up social contacts and hobbies.

The greatest possible weight should be attached to the patient's being in a position to look after himself or herself using the available technical aids. The scope of the measures required to create an environment where as little strain as possible is placed on the joints will depend to a very considerable degree on the functional capacity of the patient. With Grade II it would be sufficient to bring all heavy physical work down to one level, so that all unnecessary movement back and forth, lifting of heavy objects and carrying could be avoided. With Grade III, rather more comprehensive changes would be needed. It would be appropriate to make allowances for a possible later invalidity and to make provision at this stage for later use of a wheelchair. Patients with functional capacity of Grade IV are often forced to spend the greater part of the time in their own homes. It is therefore important for them to be able to carry out normal tasks. Household chores must often be done by a helper and in such cases, it is generally not necessary to make a lot of changes in the kitchen.

The following advice is based on an evaluation of 100 applications for alterations in the home which were processed by the Rheumatism Outpatients Centre of the University of Lund (Thorsell et al. 1984). The personnel making the home visits should preferably be supplied with check lists.

If it is necessary to make changes in the home for the patient:

- the existing home can be changed, after obtaining permission where necessary from the lessor,

- arrangements can be made for the patient to go into a nursing home,

- a new home can be built in which all the requirements can be taken into consideration.

In most cases, the first of the above alternatives will be the path chosen. In many cases, the patient will have built up a network of social contacts around himself over a long period of time and gone to great trouble to integrate with his surroundings, so that moving into a nursing home would effectively cut him off socially from the majority of his contacts, and rule out social activities such as visits to the theatre, museums and shops etc. In addition, most flats for the handicapped would still need to be adapted to the specific needs of the individual arthritic patient.

The entrance
An entrance that does not involve stairs creates more possibilities for contact with one's surroundings. For a patient confined to a wheelchair, a flight of stairs can mean complete isolation. The problem of stairs can perhaps be overcome by moving to another flat, or by installing a lift which will take a wheelchair or some other suitable equipment which would assist in negotiating the stairs, if it was not possible to find a surgical answer to the problem. Modest changes of level can often be overcome by installing a ramp.

The entrance door
Large knobs or handles and specially built-up key grips can make it easier to deal with a heavy door. It may be preferable to install electrical controls for the door.

Communication between rooms in the home
Door sills make it more difficult to get about the home in a wheelchair or on a working chair or with walking aids. If the patient has to be confined to a wheelchair, then all the doors which are not wide enough to allow the chair to pass through will have to be widened. Bathroom doors in particular are often very small. A door width of 80 cm is usually wide enough to allow a wheelchair to pass through. However, one should allow room for turning and manoeuvring the wheelchair.

Floors

Hard floors are unkind to rheumatic patients, but carpeting or even single carpets and rugs are poor alternatives. Anything that could possibly cause the patient to lose his footing and fall must be eliminated.

The balcony

A balcony or better still a terrace is an important part of a handicapped person's home. The door handle and catch should be adapted to suit the patient's needs, possibly by fitting a longer lever arm. Small ramps fitted on either side of the balcony door will give the patient easy access.

The kitchen

The kitchen should be organised in such a way that work can be carried out either sitting down or standing up. Kitchens with a breakfast corner where meals can be taken will save a great deal of walking to and fro. For patients with severe knee or hip problems it may be necessary to do the washing up sitting, unless there is a dishwasher. Taps should be replaced by single-handed mixer taps. The space requirements of such a kitchen must be particularly well adjusted to the patient's needs.

The stove

Hobs and ovens should, wherever possible, be separate. As with all equipment, it is essential to ensure that all the handles, knobs, switches, etc. can be operated by the patient without any stress on the joints.

Refrigerator and freezer

Modern refrigerators usually have an automatic defroster and are easy to take care of. The patient should try the door for himself or herself, and should attach a loop to it if the handle is not practical.

Cupboards

Many flats for the handicapped are fitted with carousel cupboards which give good utilisation of space, but can prove troublesome for rheumatic patients. A pots and pans cupboard with roller bearings, in general use today, is to be recommended.

An electrically controlled wall-mounted cupboard (**38**) permits optimum use to be made of the available space. The cupboard shown is part of the Lindgren kitchen which is particularly suitable for the handicapped. In this kitchen, the stove is accessible from two sides

126

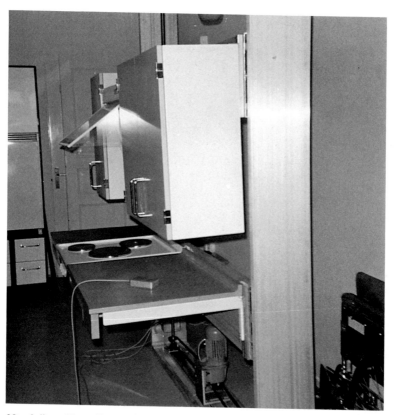

38 Adjustable wall cupboard, raised and lowered by electric motor.

and has an adjacent working surface, with the sink and its versatile taps and draining board alongside, all on one level, so that heavy pots and pans can be simply pushed backwards and forwards.

The broom cupboard
The broom cupboard should open down to floor level, so that vacuum cleaner, buckets, etc. do not need to be lifted.

The bathroom
In modern flats, the bathroom is frequently too small for a handicapped person. A great deal of thought is necessary to determine how it can be reorganised to get more room. As getting into and out of the bath is frequently very difficult, the patient may accept a shower instead of a bath. Mixer taps for hot and cold water should be fitted with thermostats. Where patients insist on having a bath, it may be

39 Kitchen working surfaces (Lindgren kitchen).

necessary to install a suitable lift, although severely handicapped polyarthritis sufferers will require a helper to assist them with bathing. Non-slip mats, a small seat to sit on in the bath and suitably placed grab rails, are so obvious as hardly to need mentioning (Thornely *et al.* 1977).

The WC should be set up higher than would normally be the case, and a seat height of 52 cm is most practical. On at least one side of the WC, but preferably on both sides, sufficient room should be left free in case one day it should become necessary to use a wheelchair in the home. Here again, solid supports, preferably detachable or swivelling, should be installed. If the patient's condition is very advanced, it might be advisable to install a Closomat (see 'Technical aids', p.121). Feminine hygiene is very much simplified by endoprosthesis of the hip joints, and also of the knee joints. In spite of that, patients with hip problems in particular, who may at some time in the future require a total prosthesis, should pay particular attention to hygiene, since infections of the urinary tract, for example, can get into the blood and set up secondary infections in the vicinity of the prosthesis causing it to become infected and loose. Furthermore, bacteria can also enter rheumatically inflamed joints via the bloodstream, which can also be dangerous.

Washing machines

For the rheumatism sufferer, who must not lift anything heavy or do any wringing out, the washing machine is the most important technical aid. The most suitable place for it would be the bathroom, unless there is a separate laundry room with spin dryer and drying cupboard.

The bedroom

Planning the bedroom and choosing the beds should take account of the fact that the patient requires contact with his or her partner. It is often easier to get into and out of bed if the bed is raised on a small platform. With twin beds, of course, both would have to be raised. Where the handicap is severe, electrically operated beds are recommended. A comfortable chair should be provided for dressing and undressing. Suitable bedclothes help with bedmaking. If a patient is dependent on a wheelchair in his or her own home, particular attention must be paid to this when designing the bedroom, so that the patient can transfer from a wheelchair straight into bed without assistance. Bedside tables should be on wheels or castors, so that they are easy to move. The clothes cupboard should also be mounted on castors, but the floor of the cupboard should remain just a few centimetres above the floor.

Summary:

Adapting the home

- Assessment of the patient's functional capacity.

- Home visit and discussion together with the family.

- Planning, with special attention to housework.

- Getting about, in the home and outside.

- Hygiene and clothes.

- Cooking and eating.

- Cleaning, washing, care of clothes.

- Sleeping and loving.

- Social contacts.

Strength training

Adapting strength and coordination to the requirements of day-to-day living and work is a part of joint protection. If the muscles are too weak or if there are any problems of coordination, as for example, between the intrinsic and extrinsic muscles of the hand, then the additional strain is taken by the ligaments and tendons, with the corresponding risk of instability and deformities occurring. The external torsion is determined by measuring the forces (tensile force × distance from axis of movement). This is equal in size to the internal torsion (contraction force of muscle × distance from axis of movement). The contraction force of the muscle fibres depends on their length and reaches its maximum when the muscle is 1.2 × the length when relaxed. Internal and external torsion vary during movement, on the one hand due to the changing muscular force and on the other hand due to the change in length of the effective lever arm.

There are two types of muscle fibre: Type I = slow contracting fibres and Type IIa and IIb = fast contracting fibres. In chronic polyarthritis, the rapidly contracting components belonging to Type II, hypotrophy (Edström and Nordemar 1974). Muscle coordination, i.e. the balancing of extensors and flexors, abductors and adductors and rotators, or of intrinsic and extrinsic muscles and their synergists, is absolutely essential for good articular function. Strength is less important for the upper extremities than for the legs, where especially the extensors of the hips, the quadriceps and the plantar flexors are essential. The abdominal muscles can play an important part in relieving the stress on the upper extremities, e.g. when getting up from lying position.

Strength training can be either static or dynamic. Both methods have advantages. Static training activates Type II fibres and can be performed in a pain-free position of the joint. However, it creates high intra-articular compression, and is not really functional training.

In dynamic strength training the intra-articular loading is changing throughout the functional range of movement. It activates both Type I and Type II fibres, and improves coordination (Grimby 1977, Nordemar 1981). Dynamic training is best performed in a warm water pool (36°C) where one can make use of the resistance of the water in special training programmes.

The damage caused by synovitis to the cartilage of the joints leads to increased friction inside the joint and increases the demand on the muscles.

The hip muscles rarely hypotrophy to the extent that strength training is called for or can be justified. Strengthening exercises for

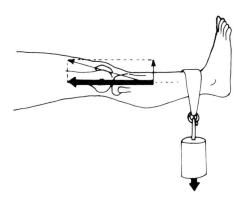

40   Quadriceps training under load conditions with an additional weight in the vicinity of the ankle. The length of the arrows is proportional to the forces created. The thrust acting on the knee is approximately 10 times as great as the weight suspended from the ankle.

the abductors in the hips causes high intra-articular compression amounting to 15 times the body weight if resistance is applied to the foot. However, strengthening of the extensors of the hip may be appropriate. This takes place with the patient lying on his back and actively raising the pelvis. A simple spring balance can be used to check the load.

Quadriceps training
As a result of pain caused by synovitides in the hip or knee joint, the muscles are inhibited. This can then lead to hypotrophy and weakness of the knee extensors. Hip pain, painful toes or ankle joints can have the same results. Functioning quadriceps muscles are necessary for the maintenance of full stability in the knee. The intra-articular stress in the knee joint during quadriceps exercises is very great. It depends on the angle of load in particular (Moritz 1977). If one loads the knee while sitting down with the knee extended, with a weight suspended from the ankle, then a compressive force 10 times as great is developed between femur and tibia through the quadriceps muscle to compensate (**40**).

The stress in the knee joint exceeds the weight of the body, even when walking on flat ground, and increases on climbing stairs. The stress depends on the height of the individual steps. The compression force reaches six times the weight of the body when the patient stands up from a sitting position (Ellis *et al.* 1979). Damage to the joint cartilage as a result of inflammatory processes, as mentioned earlier, leads to increased friction in the joint and can give rise to pain during training. Recent investigations have shown that isokinetic training, i.e. training in which the individual movements are carried out at constant speed and maximal loading through the range of movement, stresses the joint surfaces less than exercises that are carried out slowly or statically. With dynamic training one should be aware that the compression in the joint constantly changes, due to dependence of the angle of loading and the contraction force of the muscle.

Training the abdominal muscles
Strength training of the stomach muscles plays a very important role in the programme for joint protection in patients with diseased fingers and wrists, and also those suffering from elbow and shoulder trouble. If the abdominal muscles are well trained, it is possible for the polyarthritis patient to get up from a lying or sitting position with very little assistance from the upper extremities. The exercises are carried out lying down and can be made more effective through additional loading of the upper part of the body.

Hands and arms
As a rule strength training is contraindicated for the muscles of the hand and elbow, as described above (see p.41, 50). Innervation training of the extensor muscles and the intrinsic muscles, plus contracture prophylaxis, is sufficient to maintain hand functions.

Summary:

Strength training

- Up to the degree of strength required for joint function, particularly important for the abdominal muscles, and the extensor muscles of the hips and knees.

- Particularly static-isometric.

- Always taking into account the intra-articular compressing forces.

Relaxation

Many patients suffering from polyarthritis feel exhausted and live in a continual state of tiredness, though this is not due entirely to the inflammatory processes taking place in the joints. For years they have had to suppress their disappointment and desperation, with only very rare opportunities to work off their feelings and worries outwardly. The level of their ambitions in the home and at work is often unrealistically high, they are firmly resolved that the family and others around them should not suffer as a result of their disease, and the demands accordingly made by the patient on his surroundings often are far too low. The state of tension and unrest that arises from this attitude may be the reason for the state of exhaustion the patient permanently finds himself in.

In healthy people, a state of unrest and anxiety can be expressed outwardly in a variety of different ways, either in palpitations, stomach upsets or headaches on the one hand – the purely somatic reactions – or in tiredness, irritability or loss of concentration on the other hand. In the chronically sick, unrest usually manifests itself in the form of tiredness or increased susceptibility to pain (Meares 1971). This forms the background for many of the relaxation exercises which are carried out here in Lund and in Valens as part of the group therapy. Many of the patients who take part see them in a very positive light. During the treatment, the patient is comfortably seated or lying down. Suitable music or voice recordings are used to put them in a relaxed frame of mind. In most cases, we can achieve a feeling of complete peace and detachment. Conscious relaxation in daily life can raise the pain threshold and help to reduce the stress on the joints.

Joint protection in the rheumatic mother

Pregnancy, followed by the birth of the child and the new situation this creates in the home, presents a considerable upheaval in the normal life of a family. If the mother of the child is a polyarthritic, then these problems can be much more serious and call for all the assistance that the team can give (Persellin 1977, Chamberlain 1977, Östensson 1983). We know that initially, the pregnancy leads to a subjective improvement in the chronic disease. Approximately 75% of expectant mothers feel less stiff, have less swelling in the joints and are actually less tired. These changes usually occur during the first three months of pregnancy, but can also show up later. The remaining 25% of patients feel no change in their condition at all.

As a rule, the birth does not bring any specific problems relating to the inflammatory disease and the improvement usually continues for the first few weeks after the birth. Approximately 4–6 weeks after the birth, the disease becomes active again and patients find themselves going through a period of extreme tiredness, increased articular problems and more pronounced swelling in the finger and wrist joints, with pain on movement, weakness in the arms and very marked and long-drawn-out morning stiffness. This advance in the disease must be quickly recognised and dealt with, so that the functional capacity is not allowed to deteriorate.

Pregnancy is a situation not without risks for the young polyarthritic sufferer. She should be well informed as to the deterioration that can take place in her condition and she should undergo a course of instruction, together with the father, on joint protection and how to deal with the flaring up of the disease after the birth. This course of instruction can often be carried out in the form of a group discussion which includes women who have already been through such a situation and can speak from their own experience. The young mother must learn at an early stage how to take care of her child and at the same time protect her joints.

Additional aids
A few months after the birth, the ergotherapist should call on the patient, preferably while the father is at home. Patient and therapist should go through the various activities of daily living together and determine where possible difficulties could arise. For example, the patient could experience considerable pain in the wrists lifting or holding the child, or in dressing it, or when getting up in the night to attend to it, or through the increased work about the house. A comfortable chair near to the table where nappies are changed and a comfortable couch near the cradle would enable the mother to attend to the child and feed it quietly and comfortably. The therapist can also help in adapting aids and suggesting additional ones that could be of use to the young mother, and could check whether perhaps a new type of orthosis would be better. Thin bandages, and hooks and buttons should be avoided. Washing machines and dryers are decidedly more important than they are in a household without children.

Nursing
For the young arthritic mother, nursing is often a considerable strain, not only because it means having to hold back on the medication. Unless there are important reasons for not doing so, nursing should be stopped after a few months. During the entire period when she is nursing, the mother should have an opportunity to take a good rest several times a day, and if at all possible, to sleep right through the night. During this period, the father should take much more of a hand in attending to the child.

The toddler stage
The situation changes again as soon as the child starts to crawl around, to stand up and to walk independently. At this time, which usually

134

starts when the child is 1½–2 years old, the disease may still be active. In such cases, it is often very difficult for the mother to undertake all the housework, the walks in the fresh air, the washing etc. Dressing and undressing an active child can give rise to considerable pain in the hands and arms at this stage, and carrying the child becomes almost impossible. Continual monitoring, both functional and medical, and support from the entire family, are absolutely necessary if the young mother is not to become totally exhausted. Additional domestic help may also be necessary. After the first year, it may well be good for the mother to leave the child in a crèche during the day and take up some occupation, possibly on a part-time basis, so preventing the mother becoming isolated, while the child will also have an early opportunity to make social contact.

Mothers with ankylosing spondylitis usually have fewer problems, as the disease is usually much worse in men than in women. Here again, it is a matter of adopting a suitable discipline for the back, and making the necessary changes about the home at an early stage (Chamberlain 1977, Östensson 1983).

In spite of the danger of serious problems for the rheumatic mother during pregnancy, we would not wish to dissuade patients from having children, with all the joy and stimulation that bearing and bringing up a child can bring. However, we would recommend leaving 3–4 years between pregnancies. The number of children will also be limited.

Joint protection and sexual intercourse

The sex life of the polyarthritic can be upset in a number of ways. The general tiredness already mentioned, the pain, the reduced mobility and strength in the arms, hands and hips, even the fear of pain is often enough to put the partners off. Pain is the greatest barrier: it is difficult to feel like making love if one is in pain. The crises and the change in one's attitude to one's own diseased body, particularly at times when the disease is active and the condition of the joints is deteriorating, can lead to a feeling of isolation and upset relationships. The feeling of reduced self-esteem, and the uncertainties of the partner and the inhibitions, can play an important part. Free and open discussions between the partners is absolutely essential for a satisfactory solution to the problems (Greengross 1976, Boggs 1977, Hamilton 1981, Heramb 1982, Elst 1984). Analgesic medication before love-making to reduce the pain or the fear of pain may be necessary and positions would have to be changed or modified, and pillows used for support. In this context too, one might give some consideration to the possibility of endoprosthesis as a possible way of eliminating the pain and restoring mobility. A questionnaire sent out to 53 patients with an average age of 56 (20–75) who had a total hip replacement showed that with 17 of them, the sexual difficulties were fewer after the operation (Baldursson and Brattström 1979). A later investigation with a comparable number of patients showed serious deficiencies in the postoperative instruction of the patients. Careful detailed discussion with the orthopaedic surgeon or another member of the team about the problems, and the capabilities and mobility of the replaced hip is essential and would mean that patients no longer had to forgo sexual intercourse because they were afraid of what it might do to their hip. Painful, ugly and deformed hands can also be a barrier, which discussion with a psychologist, therapist, and above all a surgeon, can do much to break down.

Summary:

Joint protection for the rheumatic mother

- Careful instruction of the expectant mother and husband in joint protection.

- Check on domestic conditions 1–2 months after birth, to ascertain whether additional aids or adaptations are required.

- Short period of nursing.

- Adaptation of the home, further technical aids, specially intensive antiphlogistic therapy.

- Return to employment.

- Part-time care of the infant in a crèche.

- Active assistance with difficulties in living together.

Joint protection and earning a living

The following is based on an investigation of the situation of rheumatism sufferers who are following an occupation, carried out at the Rheumatism Outpatients Centre of the University of Lund in 1978 (Brattström and Larsson 1983/**41** and **42**/Robinson 1979). The ability to follow an occupation or profession is also affected by the disease which often strikes in middle age. Years ago, most women were solely housewives and if they were ill, this had no effect on the labour market. However, increasing numbers of women are following a vocation of some sort or other, so the situation could well change.

In the above-mentioned investigation, approximately 40% of the patients with functional capacity of Grade II were either fully employed or working part time. Most of them were employees and were not engaged in physically strenuous work. Some were bus and lorry drivers, and a few were young farmers. When making contact with patients, it is important to raise the following points at an early stage in the disease:

- Visiting the place of work.

- Simplification of certain tasks.

- Avoiding unnecessary strain at work.

- Acquiring suitable aids.

- Transport to and from the place of work.

- Organisation of domestic arrangements with the aid of other members of the family.

- Adapting the home and technical equipment at home.

- Reduction in working hours, possibly part-time or half-day working, with reduced pension.

- Retraining as a last resort.

The investigation shows an uncommonly low rate of absenteeism for patients with chronic polyarthritis or ankylosing spondylitis (see **41** and **42**). The most obvious explanation for this would be the enhanced motivation of the patients employed on work that is not physically demanding, and perhaps also the feeling that they have to do better than the others because of their illness. In many cases, part-time working is very beneficial because it gives them a measure of social contact and an opportunity to keep their minds on other things, rather than their own specific problems. Their body and the disease no longer become the central feature in their lives. Finally, the daily contact with other people gives them new ideas and fresh stimulation in the form of new interests (see **30**). This shows how a 32-year-old polyarthritic patient got to grips with her particular situation over a period of 10 years and how her personality developed as a result (Heramb 1979, personal communication).

Patient education

As mentioned earlier in the book, the knowledge and understanding patients have of their disease and their acceptance of the disease are important factors in maintaining their functional capacity over a long period of time (Swezey and Swezey 1976, Vignos *et al.* 1972, 1976, Althoff and Nordenskiöld 1985, del Bueno 1978). It is therefore important that part of the treatment should aim to impart a knowledge of the course of the disease and of the methods of treating it. This instruction should be structured according to the patient's motivation, level of education and the facilities available for the

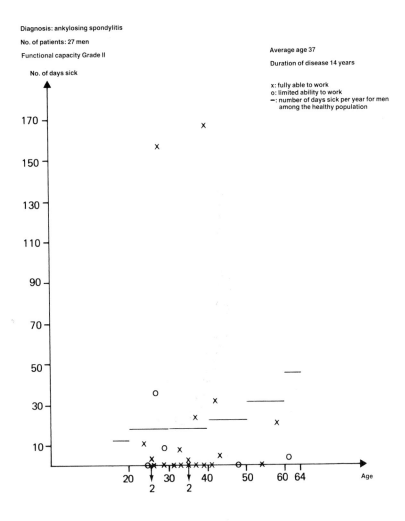

41 Number of days sick per year for patients with ankylosing spondylitis compared with the healthy population (Brattström and Larsson 1983).

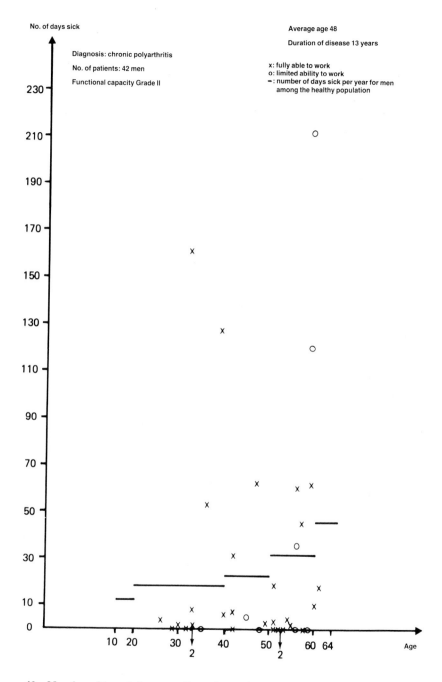

42 Number of days sick per year for patients with chronic polyarthritis compared with the healthy population (Brattström and Larsson 1983).

purpose. This type of communication represents the most important part of the entire treatment. Instruction calls for patient motivation, but it is difficult to continue motivating patients once they have been discharged from hospital after a short period of hospital treatment and have returned home. The patient should be ready and willing to keep acquiring new knowledge which could help him to master the problems of his day-to-day life. This compliance will not be present until the patient has accepted the fact that he is suffering from a disease that will be with him all his life. However, it will not be possible to accept a new way of life until it is clear to the patient that it can lead to improvements. It is therefore essential to measure the effects of treatment in order to be able to prove to the patient that the effort has been worthwhile and has produced results.

Continuous monitoring of the patient and the results of the instructions, are necessary to make sure that the patient keeps up the training exercises, especially since the patient is under threat of a further deterioration. The compliance is discussed and the results of education are not always lasting (Belcon *et al.* 1984, Parker *et al.* 1984).

A training programme implies that one must be clear:

- which group of people the instruction is aimed at,

- what the objectives are,

- what material will be used,

- how one will determine the results of the measures taken.

In the Rheumatism Outpatients Centre in Lund, we have a systematic course of instruction for patients, usually in groups of 4–5, which lasts a total of 20 hours, usually spread over a week with 4 hours' instruction per day. The teachers are the team members: ergotherapist (E), physiotherapist (PT), nurse (N), social worker (S) and the doctor (D). All of them are fully informed as to the specific situation of each of the patients. The aim is to increase their sense of security by imparting the following knowledge:

- Prognosis and critical moments in the disease (D, N, E, PT).

- Effects and side-effects of the principal medicaments (D, N).

- Joint protection including simple biomechanical facts regarding loading the joints in daily life (PT, E).

- Contractures, their development and prophylaxis (PT, E).

- Muscle training as part of a way of life aimed at protecting the joints (PT, E).

- Technical aids and orthoses for protecting the joints (PT, E).

- Techniques of relaxation (PT).

- Social assistance in adapting the home, in training, etc. (S, E).

- Positive attitude towards seeking compensation in other fields, such as hobbies etc. (all together).

The instruction is divided up into theory and practice, with plenty of opportunity for discussion among the patients. A conscious effort is made to include the experience of the individual patients in the course of instruction. The regular evaluation of the skills, mobility and strength after the course is completed gives the patients a measure of confirmation of what has gone before (Brattström *et al.* 1980).

This book and various books of instruction put out by the Swedish Rheumatism Association are used as a basis for this instruction (Althoff *et al.* 1985). The publications of the Rheumatism Association are sent to the patients a few weeks before the course, so that they can do a certain amount of preliminary study on the topics to be discussed. A scientific evaluation of the results of this work over a long period will be needed to show whether we are on the right path.

As psychological problems are often of importance to the patients, group psychotherapy may in the future become more common (Kaplan and Kozin 1981).

Summary: the team approach

Integrated rehabilitation of chronically ill polyarthritic patients is possible provided one can get together a team capable of planning the various medical, functional and social measures and combining them in such a way that they meet the needs of the patients (Berglund 1979, Feinburg 1984). In the final instance, the decisions are left to the patient.

Surgical intervention has achieved considerable importance in maintaining functional capacity in chronic polyarthritis sufferers, which is one reason why an orthopaedic surgeon specialising in rheumatic disorders and a hand surgeon are part of the team. The planning of operations and postoperative rehabilitation is a matter for the entire group, but here again, the final decision is left to the patient. A high degree of ability to feel their way into the patient's world and psyche is demanded of all the team. One must respect the patient's aims and at the same time be ready to give expert advice and to convince him.

Establishing and formulating the objectives of the treatment and planning the steps necessary for their implementation always concludes with a detailed discussion of the necessary means and medication, operations or technical aids. The end result can often only be reached in stages. The requirements of the patients at home provide both the scale and the direction for all these planning measures, as well as their requirements at work, in getting about and in preventing any further progress on the part of the disease and the accompanying complications. The following list of sensible objectives and possible measures at various stages of the disease will serve as a summary of what we have already discussed.

Objectives and measures at various stages of the disease

General summary

Objectives in functional capacity Grades I and II
- Reduction of feelings of insecurity and anxiety.
- Checking of activity of the disease and of pain.
- Knowledge of contracture prophylaxis and joint protection.
- Maintaining previous activities in the home and at work.

Measures in functional capacity Grades I and II
- Diagnostic examination.
- Information.
- Careful medical treatment (non-steroidal anti-inflammatory drugs).
- Joint protection.
- Contracture prophylaxis.
- Technical aids to relieve strain and alleviate pain, possibly orthosis.

Objectives in functional capacity Grade II (risk class)
- Adapting to the disease.
- Reducing the activity of the disease and the pain.
- Maintaining mobility and strength.
- Maintaining independence.
- Adapting to a cautious and protective way of life.
- Stimulation of new interests.
- Tightening the family bonds.

- Maintaining the ability to work for a living.
- Avoiding the risks.

Measures in functional capacity Grade II (risk class)

Doctor's certificate only for short period of time, i.e. only off work through sickness for a short period of time.

- Basic treatment with chloroquine, gold and penicillamine, etc.

- Precise information on effects and side-effects of medicaments.

- Steroid injections in the joints or local infiltrations, especially in the region of the tendon sheaths, tendons and tendon insertions.

- Treatment of any complications that arise.

- Preventive hand surgery and preventive orthopaedic rheumatic surgery, such as synovectomy, tenosynovectomy and tenotomy.

- Group instruction and information for family and helpers.

- Helping the patient to accept the disease.

- Principles of joint protection in everyday life and at work.

- Stress-relieving aids and splints.

- Contracture prophylaxis.

- Training the quadriceps and extensor muscles of the hip.

- Bodily hygiene, feet and teeth.

- Precise information on social assistance.

- Stress-relieving exercises in the pool.

- Adapting the home including the kitchen equipment and equipping with household machines, washing machines, dryers, etc.

- Technical aids in the bathroom.

- Contacts and adaptations at work.

- Help with solving transport problems.

- Extending social contacts, new interests.

- Involving the family in all activities.

Objectives in functional capacity Grade III

- Most effective possible alleviation of pain.
- Maintaining existing contacts.
- Spare-time activities and hobbies.
- Maintaining certain standards in everyday life and ability to walk and get around.
- Maintaining the ability to do some housework.

Measures in functional capacity Grade III

- Attenuation of inflammatory activity.
- Attention to and avoidance of possible complications.
- Instruction and psychological support, also of family.
- Financial assistance.
- Instruction of family members in contracture prophylaxis and quadriceps training.
- Regular physiotherapy for limited periods.
- Applying the principles of joint protection.
- Intensive bodily hygiene (teeth, feet, feminine hygiene).
- Mechanical equipment and aids as in Grade II (risk class).
- Wheelchair for travelling longer distances.
- Orthopaedic hand surgery.
- Adapting the home.
- Occasional visits to spas, courses of treatment.
- Increased social contacts and interests.

Objectives in functional capacity Grade III with threat of falling to Grade IV

- Optimal alleviation of pain.
- Getting the patient out of the risk zone.
- Maintaining some ability to walk, however slight.
- Reduction of complete dependence on others in everyday life.
- Best possible domestic atmosphere.
- Keeping hobbies and existing contacts.

Measures in functional capacity Grade III with threat of falling to Grade IV

As with functional capacity Grade III, but in addition continuous orthopaedic and surgical monitoring.

- Reconstructive and pain-relieving surgery.

- Plastic joint surgery, especially in the region of the hip, knee, hand and finger joints.

- Possible late synovectomy of the knee.

- Contracture-prophylactic surgery.

Attention: Postoperative rehabilitation in every case.
Treatment of medical complications.
Intensive hygiene (teeth, feet, feminine hygiene).
Suitable attenuation of the activity of the disease.
Adapting the home and special technical equipment.

- Electrically controlled bed, lift, wheelchair for use outside the home.

- Special financial assistance, possibly special taxi for handicapped people.

Objectives in functional capacity Grade IV
- Optimum alleviation of pain.
- Keeping the patient in his or her own home.
- Independent locomotion.
- With hospitalisation, occasional discharge to return home for a while.

Measures in functional capacity Grade IV
- Constant monitoring for impending or manifest medical complications.

- Adapting the surroundings.

- Maximum economic support.

- Aids to replace damaged functions as in functional capacity Grade III (risk patients).

- Special aids (push-button telephone, electric door opener, further devices for environmental control).

Part III
ILLUSTRATED SECTION

Cutting – eating – drinking

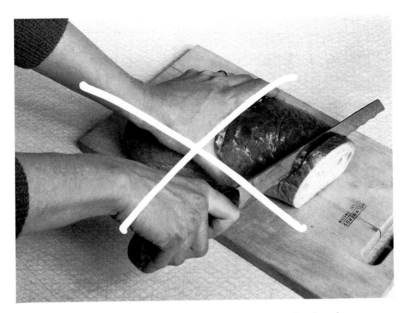

Wrong: Gripping the handle of the knife firmly when cutting bread, sausage or cheese. The fingers are forced outwards towards the ulna.

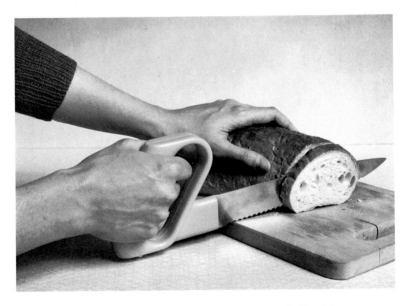

Right: If a special knife with a suitably adapted handle is used – 23 × 34 mm, set at an angle of 60° to the blade – the effort required to control the blade is greatly reduced.

Best of all: Avoid any strain whatsoever on the finger joints by using a bread slicer. There are hand-operated and electrically driven slicers. The handle can be lengthened and increased in size with a foam-rubber sleeve. In addition, there are many different kinds of sliced bread available in the shops!

Wrong: Pressing down on the cheese cutter with the index finger, forcing the other fingers outwards.

Right: The handle is adapted to the rheumatic hand. The pressure is applied to the fingers and the wrist at right angles. The effort required to hold the cutter steady is small. (Model: I. Jönsson, Outpatients Rehabilitation Centre, University of Lund.)

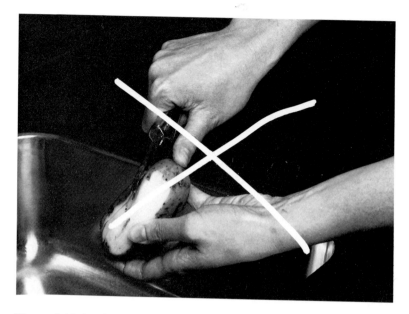

Wrong: A kitchen knife or potato peeler should never be gripped firmly with the fingers. This sets up considerable forces in the MCP joints, acting in the direction of the palm.

Right: A potato peeler with a large soft handle requires less effort and reduces the unavoidable stress on the MCP and PIP joints.

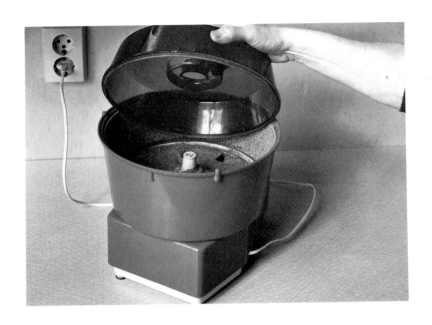

Best of all: Change the method. Use a potato peeling machine – lengthen the handle and increase its size with a foam-rubber sleeve.

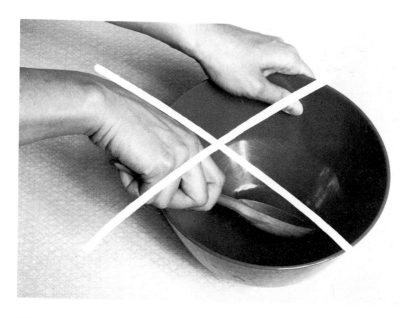

Wrong: Grasping the handle of the wooden spoon tightly, forcing the fingers outwards.

Right: Increase the size of the handle with foam-rubber or some other suitable soft material and, if possible, use a mixing machine.

Wrong: Holding a heavy cup with the tips of the fingers.

Right: Lifting a two-handled plastic beaker with both hands.

154

Right: Cup made of lightweight transparent plastic, beaker consisting of glass and holder, and melamine plate with a rim so that food can be pushed against it (designed by Benktzon and Juhlin).

Right: A glass with a large pedestal and thick stem is comfortable to hold and easier to lift. The bell-shaped top section rests on the top of the hand. The low weight and shorter distance to travel are additional advantages.

Cutlery

Special knife, fork and spoon

The handle of the knife fits comfortably into the hand and enables the user to cut with the wrist slightly extended. Normally, a push–pull action is used in cutting, but this knife can also be used with a rocking action, for which the food being cut does not need to be held so firmly. This is very important when only one hand can be used for cutting. The rounded blade of the knife makes it unnecessary to alter the angle between the blade and the handle (Benktzon and Juhlin 1984).

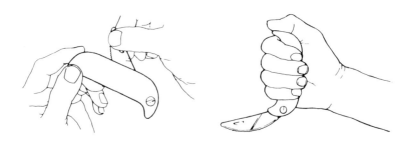

The specially thick handles of the fork and spoon make them easier to grasp in the palm of the hand. The greatly rounded bottom end avoids the creation of pressure points in the palm. The elliptical cross section is another factor which helps to stabilise the hand (Benktzon and Juhlin 1984).

Cutlery with thick, soft, light handles of plastic covered with cork (Outpatient Rehabilitation Centre, Lund).

Lifting

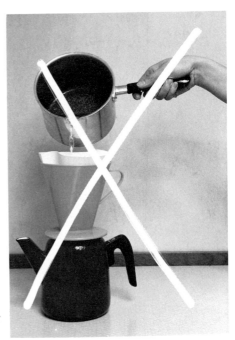

Wrong: Lifting heavy pots or kettles.

Right: Adapt the method. Use a lighter pot and reduce the strain on the MCP and PIP joints and the wrist.

Wrong: Trying to lift a heavy pot in this way.

Right: Change the method. Take a long-handled fork and lift the potatoes out one by one.

Right: Cook the potatoes and other vegetables in a pot with a basket or built-in strainer.

Wrong: Stressing the wrist and MCP joints by lifting heavy frying pans, coffee pots, trays, etc.

Right: Take the strain on the lower arm, which is stronger and usually pain-free.

Wrong: Stressing the MCP and PIP joints of the fingers when lifting piles of plates, for example.

Wrong: The same applies when lifting a tray in this way.

Right: If it is absolutely essential to carry anything, then the more joints or groups of joints used together, the better. In this example, the PIP and MCP joints and the wrists are all used, thus spreading the load. This does, however, call for unimpaired and pain-free supination of the forearms, a movement which is important in so many other aspects of daily life.

Best of all: Change the method. Remove all the door sills and use a small serving trolley, effectively avoiding all unnecessary strain.

Opening bottles, tins and jars

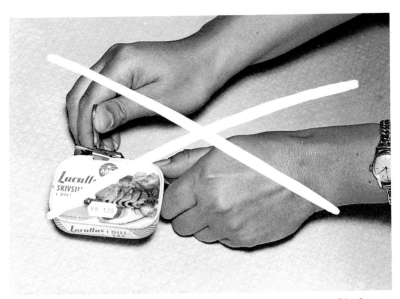

Wrong: Using a tin opener operated by pressure applied by the top part of the fingers. This puts strain on the thumb joints, as well as the MCP and PIP joints of all the fingers.

Right: Use a wall-mounted tin opener, fixed at elbow height. By lengthening the handle and padding it with a suitable soft material, unnecessary strain on the joints of the fingers can be avoided.

Wrong: Undoing a screw-type lid in this way. This puts a heavy strain on the MCP joints, forcing them outwards in ulnar direction.

Right: Use both hands together, clamping the lid of the jar firmly in a suitable device and turning with the entire body, without stressing or moving the wrists or elbows. The device must, of course, be mounted at a suitable height.

Right: Cutting board and holding aid designed to replace the function of a second hand in food preparation. The board has an adjustable clamp and a reversible plate with nails for peeling and slicing.

169

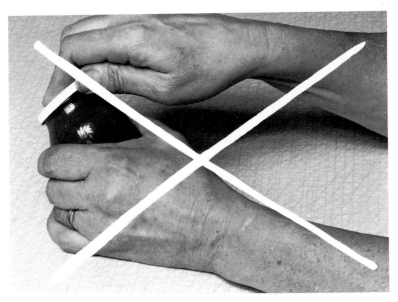

Wrong: Exerting pressure on the thumb to lift the lid of a jar.

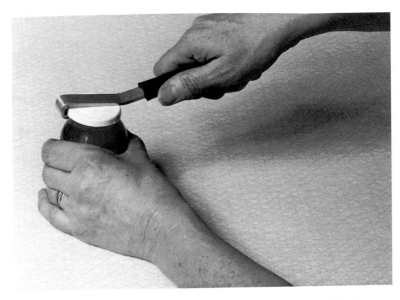

Right: Use an opener with a long thick handle, taking advantage of the leverage (Outpatients Rehabilitation Centre, Lund, I. Jönsson).

Wrong: Exerting pressure with the top part of the fingers to open a bottle.

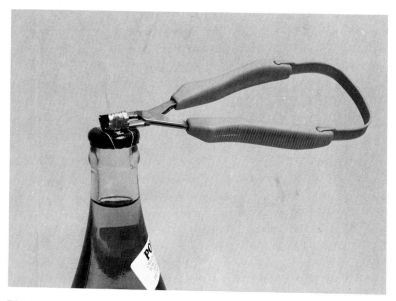

Right: This opener has a sprung grip and can be operated with the hand relatively wide open, thus removing much of the strain.

Wrong: Putting strain on eroded MCP joints by turning stiff taps on and off. The pressure required from the top part of the fingers, coupled with the pronounced ulnar drift, involves quite unnecessary risks.

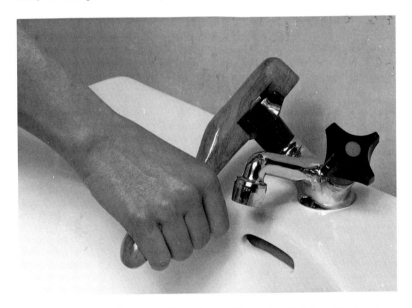

Right: A suitable implement can be used to avoid stressing the joints. The long lever arm reduces the amount of effort required. Each such implement must be adapted to one particular type of tap. Unfortunately, there are all too many of them.

Miscellaneous manual operations

Right: Single-handed mixer taps come in a wide variety of different forms.

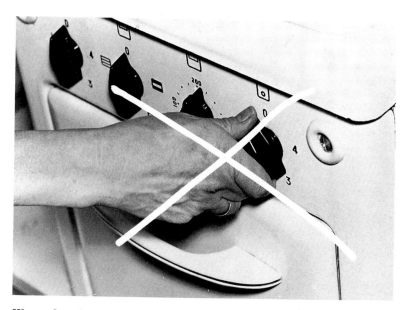

Wrong: Stressing the MCP joints with ulnar stress when operating a switch.

Right: Use a suitable implement to keep the effort required to a minimum.

175

Wrong: Applying pressure in the wrong direction to painful MCP joints when locking a door: in this example, extrinsic minus deformity in the case of the thumb and ulnar drift in the case of the MCP joint of the index finger.

Right: The universal grip (Pigge) makes it easier to turn small keys and door catches.

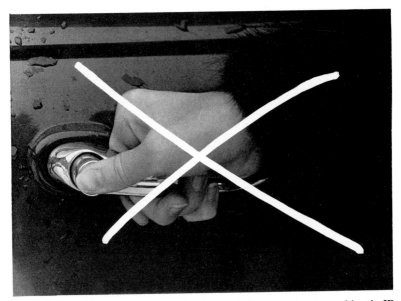

Wrong: Outward pressure on the MCP joints of the fingers and overstretching the IP joint of the thumb when opening a car door.

Right: Polyarthritis sufferers often have trouble with car doors. This implement fits round the handle and pushes the button in when a small amount of leverage is applied. Similar implements can also be used on other types of doors, for example, on certain types of refrigerator (Outpatients Rehabilitation Centre, Lund. G. Persson).

Other manual operations

Wrong: Wringing out a dish-cloth. All the joints in the hands and fingers are subjected to very heavy stress.

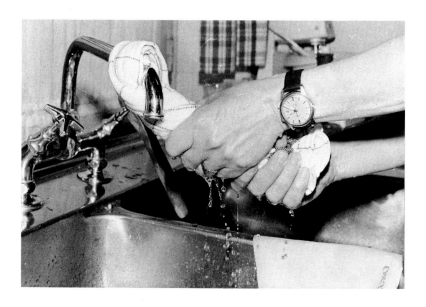

Right: The dish-cloth can be looped round a tap and twisted.

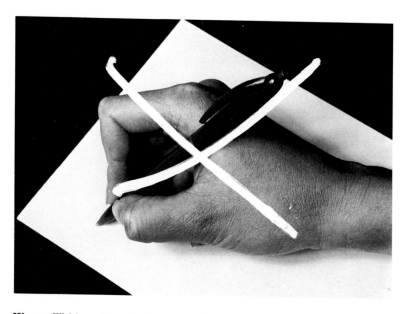

Wrong: Writing with a slender pen requires considerable finger pressure and puts great strain on the MCP and IP joints of the thumb and index finger.

Right: A thick grip, preferably of foam rubber, protects the joints. Felt-tip pens are also recommended.

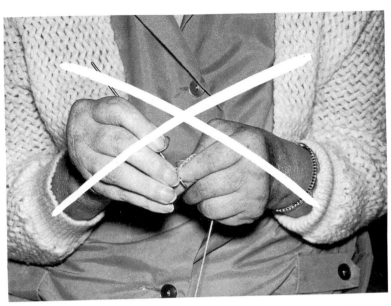

Wrong: It is not difficult to see that crocheting with a thin needle is extremely bad for the fingers.

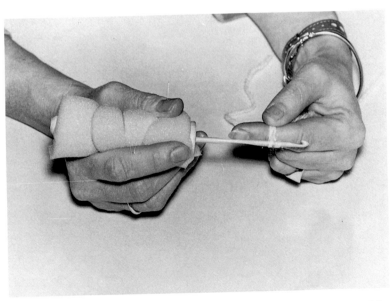

Right: Thickening the bottom end of the needle considerably reduces stress and the pressure required of the muscles of the hand and fingers. If important to the patient the activity should be continued.

182

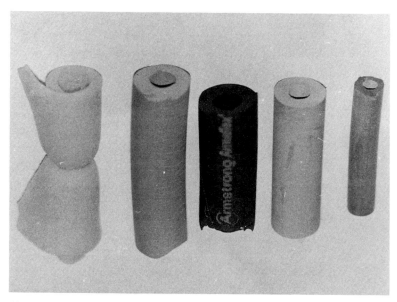

Sleeves and wads of foam rubber in varying thicknesses can be used wherever a soft thick handle is required and increased surface friction needed to give a better grip.

Sitting

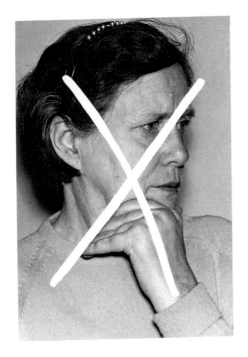

Wrong: Propping one's head up in such a way that the weight pushes the fingers outwards.

Wrong: Propping one's head up in any way that puts pressure on the fingers.

186

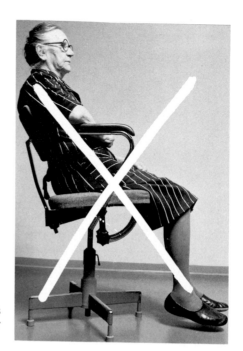

Wrong: Sitting with the knees bent and insufficient support for the feet.

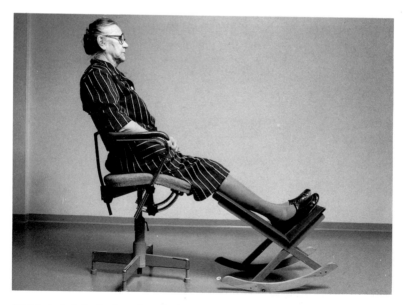

Right: A chair for both work and relaxation, with adjustable armrests and backrest and split seat (Bimax model). 'Rocking chair' type foot rest to support the feet. Especially suitable for patients with reduced mobility in hips and knees.

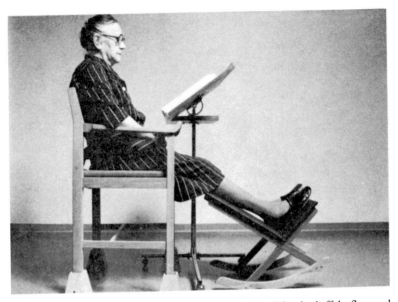

Right: Chair with comfortably adjusted armrests. The chair is raised off the floor and the patient's knees are stretched, while the feet are supported on the foot rest. The reading table is mounted on castors and can easily be moved.

Right: Adjustable reading stand.

Right: Chair with adjustable split seat (Bimax chair) or asymmetric cushion (below) which is soft on one side. These seats provide great relief for patients with stiff knees or pronounced loss of flexion in the hip joints.

Saddle-shaped chair: A working chair with adjustable back support to relieve the hip and knee joints. The seat, shaped like a motorcycle saddle, eases the hip joints into a slightly abducted position and when set at the correct height, permits the hip joints to be almost fully stretched. A suitable foot rest is also required.

Various types of chair
The 'Realstuhl' models (left and right) are used predominantly in Sweden. This model has adjustable armrests, backrest and seat, runs on wheels and is fitted with an extra-long brake lever. The chair in the centre is a saddle-shaped chair.

190

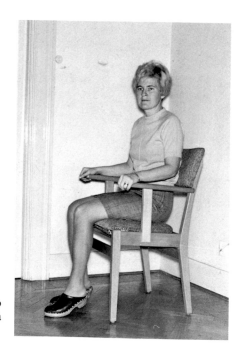

Right: Patients with painful hip and knee joints should sit on a higher chair than usual.

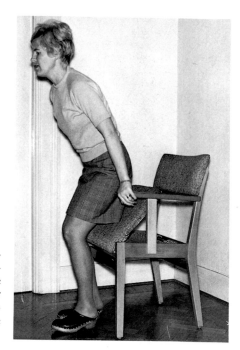

Right: Patients with weak quadriceps muscles or extremely painful and/or unstable hip and knee joints may find an ejector chair very useful. Nowadays, electrically operated ejector chairs are often preferred.

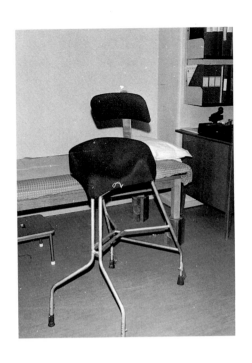

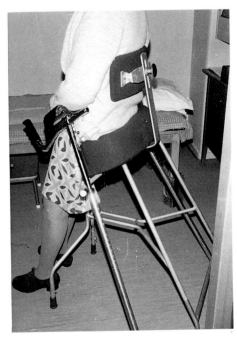

Working chair specially made from plaster casts for a patient with hip and knee joints stiffened in an extended position (Outpatients Rehabilitation Centre, Lund. G. Persson).

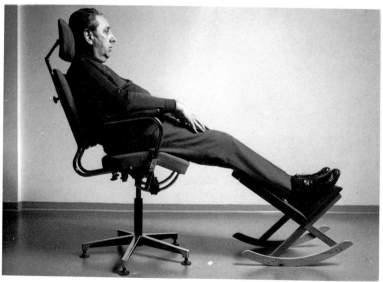

Right: The Bimax coxarthrosis chair with headrest and split seat is the answer to the problems of the ankylosing spondylitis patient with a stiff and painful neck and seriously impaired mobility in the hip joints.

Wrong: When standing up from a chair, the joints of the fingers and the wrists are subjected to stress, depending on the positioning of the hands.

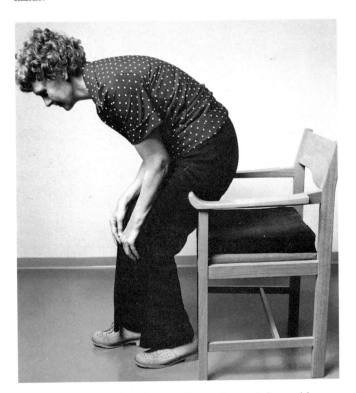

Right: The correct action when standing up from a sitting position – incline the head and upper part of the body forwards, thus transferring the centre of gravity forwards, and place one foot slightly in front of the other. In this way, the effort required of the extensor muscles of the hip and knee joints is greatly reduced.

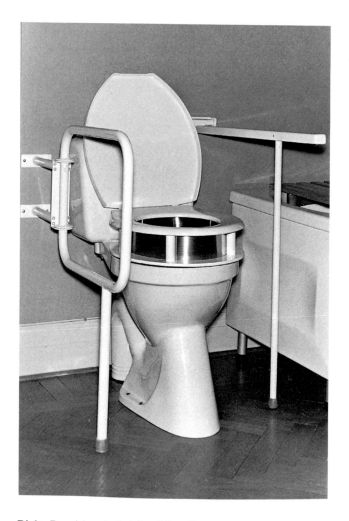

Right: By raising the height of the toilet seat and providing various types of safety frame and grab bar, either fixed or retractable, the stress on the patient's knee and hip joints on sitting down and standing up can be greatly reduced.

Lying

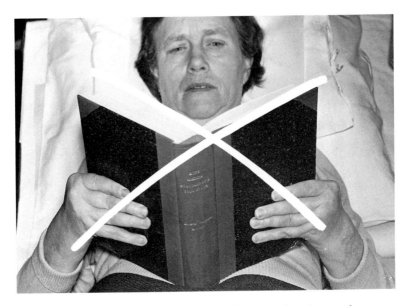

Wrong: Holding a book in such a way that the fingers are forced outwards.

Right: Use a reading table or book support.

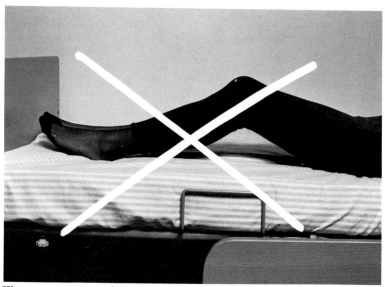

Wrong: As a result of primary flexion contracture in the hip joint, secondary compensatory flexion contracture occurs in the knee joint and vice versa. Where arthritis is present in the ankle joints, this can rapidly lead to footdrop (fixed plantar flexion).

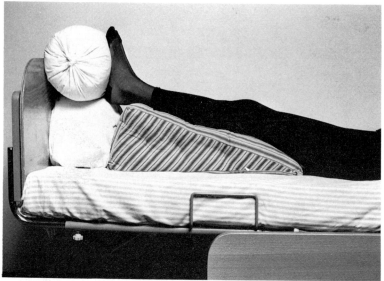

Right: If the primary contracture is in the hip region, then secondary flexion contracture in the knee can be prevented by a wedge-shaped bolster. However, it is important that the feet should be in the neutral position, at a slight angle to the lower leg, and suitably supported in this position.

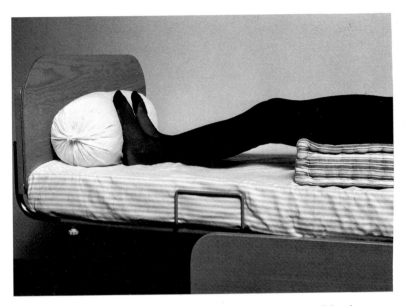

Right: If the impaired extension is primarily in the knee, then an additional mattress under the back and seat can help to prevent loss of secondary extension in the hip joint.

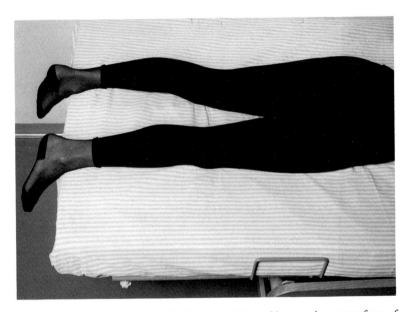

Right: The abdominal position with both legs abducted is a very important form of contracture prophylaxis. It is designed to prevent adduction contracture and footdrop. The feet must be able to hang down over the bottom end of the bed.

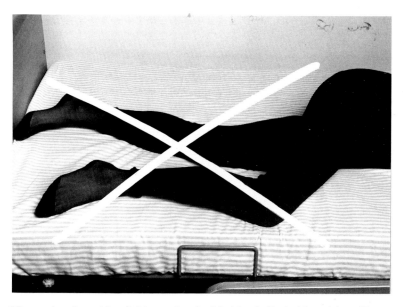

Wrong: A patient with arthritis or arthrosis of the hip who lies in this position will very soon suffer adduction contracture and impaired extension.

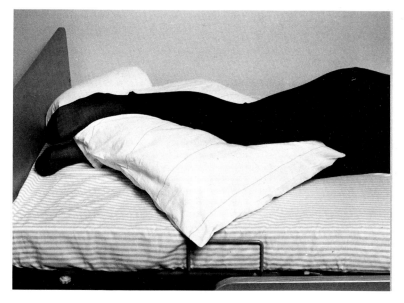

Right: Adduction contracture can be avoided by never allowing the legs to become crossed. A cushion or pillow placed between the knees is sufficient.

Aids to walking

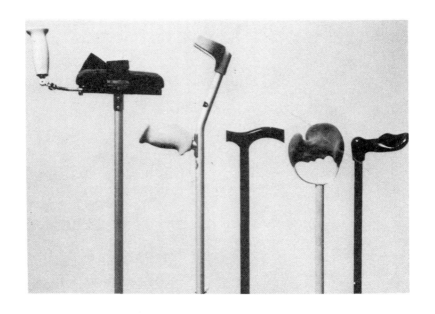

Various types of sticks and crutches.

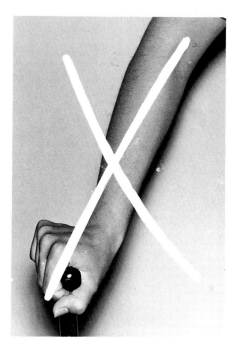

Wrong: The stick is too long and the wrist is over-extended. With this position, any arthritis in the wrist would rapidly become worse.

Right: While taking the patient's weight, the wrist must at all costs be kept in the neutral position.

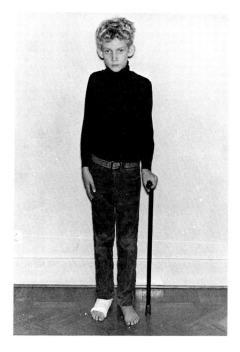

Correct stick length. The stick should be carried on the opposite side to the painful joint.

205

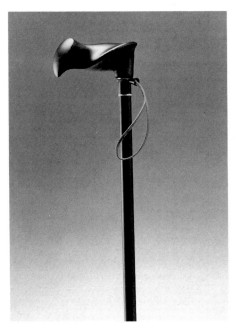

Walking stick for people with limited hand–arm function. The design is characterised by: larger load-bearing areas for the hand; the handle has an adjustable angle (ball and socket joint); good friction between hand and handle with a soft surface; a handle that allows the fingers to be flexed together; low weight; and a plastic wrist strap (Ergonomi Design Gruppen, Sweden).

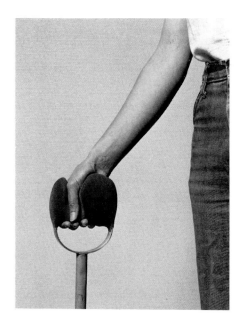

Right: A handle specially designed from plaster casts for a patient with very severe polyarthritic deformities of the hand and fingers (Outpatients Rehabilitation Centre, Lund. G. Persson).

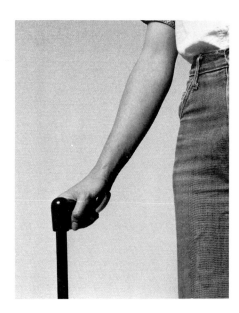

Right: Walking stick with plateau-shaped handle which distributes the weight over the entire surface of the palm.

207

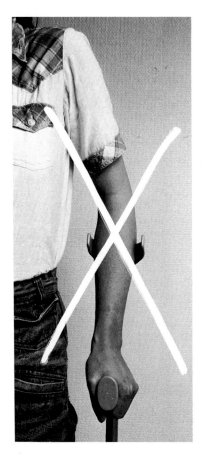
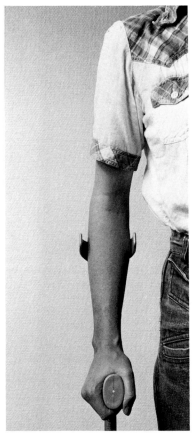

Wrong: This elbow crutch is too long, leading to excessive stressing of elbow and wrist. In order to get anything like sufficient support, the patient must allow his shoulder to be pushed upwards by the crutch.

Right: The weight is transferred to the wrist and elbow along the line of the arm, and the shoulder remains in the normal position.

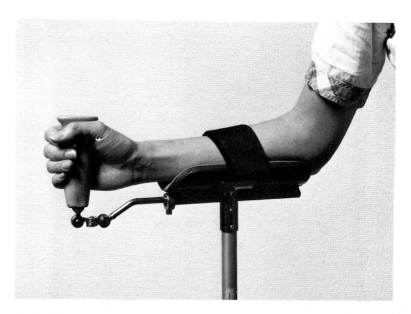

Right: This forearm crutch – or Althoff crutch – has a grip that can be adjusted in three different planes, thereby making it possible to adjust very precisely to deformities in the hand.

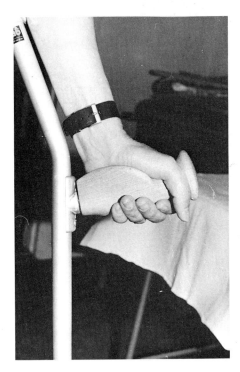

Right: Thick, machine-turned grip individually adapted to the patient's hand.

PATIENT INSTRUCTION SHEETS

The following pages form the cornerstone of the instruction programme we use to help our patients with their daily life. The instruction we give is based on the basic knowledge acquired by the patients from a careful study of the literature we send them. In German-speaking countries, we make particular use of this book and the explanatory literature produced by the Swiss Rheumatism Association. Over the past few years, a steady stream of new instructional literature has appeared to help people suffering from polyarthritis, as well as their families and helpers. For further information, they should turn to their doctors, therapists, social workers or the nearest branch of their regional Rheumatism Association (Arthritis Care in the UK).

Naturally, our programme can be modified to take account of existing or potentially available facilities.

Staff of the Rheumatism Outpatients Centre, Lund

Staff of the Medical Department, Bad Ragaz
and the Rheumatism and Rehabilitation Clinic, Valens

Inflamed joint, early stage

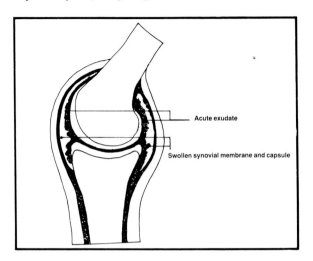

Acute exudate

Swollen synovial membrane and capsule

Inflamed joint, late stage

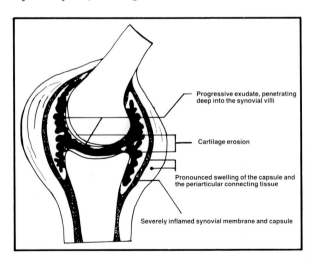

Progressive exudate, penetrating deep into the synovial villi

Cartilage erosion

Pronounced swelling of the capsule and the periarticular connecting tissue

Severely inflamed synovial membrane and capsule

The joints of the upper and lower extremities are in principle the same in structure.

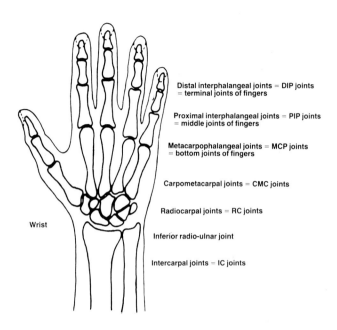

Distal interphalangeal joints = DIP joints
= terminal joints of fingers

Proximal interphalangeal joints = PIP joints
= middle joints of fingers

Metacarpophalangeal joints = MCP joints
= bottom joints of fingers

Carpometacarpal joints = CMC joints

Radiocarpal joints = RC joints

Inferior radio-ulnar joint

Intercarpal joints = IC joints

Wrist

Schematic diagram of hand

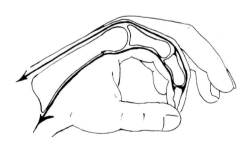

Schematic diagram of hand gripping object between tips of index finger and thumb, showing extensor digitorum communis and flexor digitorum sublimis

213

Anatomy of the upper extremities

Thoracic girdle Breastbone, collar bone, shoulder blade, upper arm and the joints connecting these bones

Elbow Joints between upper arm on the one side and ulna and radius on the other

Hand tendons The extensor tendons of the back of the hand and the flexor tendons of the palm of the hand

Muscles Proceeding from the lower arm and attaching to the bones of the hand and fingers = extrinsic muscles
Points of origin and attachment both in the area of the bones of the hand and fingers = intrinsic muscles

Nerves Median nerve
Ulnar nerve
Radial nerve

Functional mobility

Grasps Finger-tip grasp: between thumb and tip of index finger

Key grasp: between extended thumb and radial surface of bent index finger

Cylindrical grasp: involving powerful flexing of middle, ring and little fingers in the case of slender cylindrical objects, and including the index finger and thumb in the case of larger cylindrical objects

Forearm and wrist Rotary movements:
palm uppermost = supination
palm downwards = pronation

214

Range of action of hand	Leading to the mouth, the face, the chest, the neck, the back, the lower abdomen and the anus

Development of deformities:

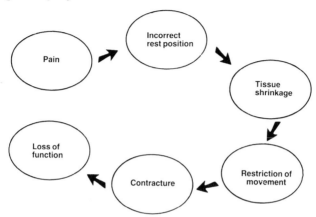

Changes in the upper extremities in inflammatory diseases of the joints

Pain

Restriction of movement

Shoulder	Especially important, restriction of rotation and movement of the upper arm away from the body
Elbow	Restriction of bending Restriction of stretching
Elbow and hand combination	Restriction of rotation of the hand in the horizontal axis
Wrist	Restriction of stretching and bending

Deformities

Hand and finger joints	*Subluxation* of the bottom finger joints: the surfaces of the joint slip relative to one another, so that the finger joint surfaces move in the direction of the palm. In particularly severe cases, the surfaces of the joints can cease to be congruent, in which case it is termed luxation

Ulnar deviation: the index, middle and ring fingers are bent over towards the little finger at the bottom joints (ulnar drift)

Inability to clench the fist

Shoemaker's thumb: the thumb is bent outwards

Weakness　Partially the result of insufficient use due to pain caused by the inflammatory changes, and partially due to involvement of the muscles, tendons and tendon sheaths in the inflammatory rheumatic process, or also through damage to the cartilage or bone

When do deformities develop in the hand?

Internal stress with the finger-tip and cylindrical grasps

Finger-tip grasp: if one grasps an object, such as a pencil or needle, in this way, the flexor tendons shown in black in the diagram are contracted.

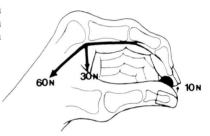

Cylindrical grasp: the same action is involved if an object is gripped tightly, with all the fingers of the hand bent round it.

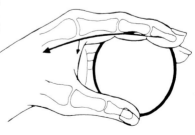

216

Owing to the position of the flexor tendons and the anatomy of the area surrounding the bottom joints of the fingers, excessive stress can jeopardise the stability of these joints. Deformities, subluxations and luxations of the small bones in the finger joints are potential consequences. The volar pressure acting on the bottom joints of the fingers is more than three times as great as the force exerted by the grasp.

External stresses: Any rotary movement in which the fingers are forced in the direction of the ulna – i.e. towards the little finger – as in lifting, holding a book when reading, writing, driving in screws, turning a key, turning taps, etc.

Joint protection and relieving the strain on the upper extremities

How can one prevent deformities developing?

- Treat the inflammation: medicaments, local injections of anti-inflammatory compounds originally derived from cortisone whose side-effects have now been reduced to a minimum, functional splints and rest splints.

- Contracture prophylaxis through regular programmes of stress-free exercises. Body exercises in warm water, best of all in a kinotherapeutic bath or swimming pool. Physiotherapy with a fully qualified physiotherapist.

- Regular vigorous exercises for the stomach muscles.

- Reduction of the forces acting on the joints by:
  – increasing the size of handles and padding them,
  – using longer levers and favourable angles of stress,
  – spreading the load over several joints or groups of joints,
  – taking heed of pain and avoiding wherever possible,
  – working for shorter periods, adapting working methods,
  – adaptive devices,
  – adapting working surroundings.

Contracture prophylaxis in the region of the upper extremities

(modified after Althoff and Nordenskiöld 1977)

Every joint should be exercised and gently worked at least once a day. For the patient suffering from chronic polyarthritis, this should become as much a part of the daily routine as, for example, cleaning one's teeth. The individual exercises can easily be spaced out over the whole day. They should be performed slowly and should not cause any pain. Don't forget to take a break now and then! Many of the exercises can be performed lying down on a couch or bed. Relaxation is helped by gentle and rhythmic abdominal breathing. In some cases, instruction in relaxation may be necessary from a physiotherapist, or from a tape.

Shoulder exercises performed lying down

- Bend your elbows and try to move your upper arms away from the body until they are at right angles to it.

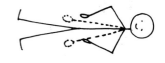

- Clasp your hands and bend your arms, then raise the arms over the head with arms bent, then unclasp the hands and with the arms still raised, straighten the elbows, then swing the outstretched arms away from the body and back together again, then return to the starting position. During these exercises, pain must be avoided; if that is not possible, only those parts of the exercise which can be performed without pain should be carried out, or the exercise should be omitted altogether.

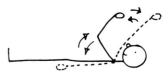

Elbows

- With the upper arms resting on the bed, bend the elbows at right angles

so that the forearms are perpendicular to the body. In this position, rotate the forearms so that you are alternately looking at the palm and back of the hands.

- Bend the elbows as far as possible and then stretch them again. In the extended position, the back of the hand is uppermost, while in the bent position, the palm of the hand is turned towards the face.

Shoulder exercises performed sitting down

- First sit down on a suitable chair and let the arms hang down loosely.

- In this position, go through the normal range-of-motion exercises: move the hand to the neck, the forehead and the mouth, scratch yourself between the shoulder blades, comb your hair, etc.

Shoulder exercises performed standing up

- A painful shoulder can be exercised by inclining the upper part of the body forwards in a standing position and allowing the arm to swing gently to and fro. The further forward one leans, the greater the amount of movement possible at the shoulder.

- After completing this exercise, sit down with the forearms resting on a table and relax for a while, paying particular attention to the shoulders, shoulder girdle and neck.

Wrists

- Clench the fist and incline the hand from the wrist in the direction of the little finger without moving the forearm. Then flex the fingers. Now bring the hand back to the starting position. Never incline the hand towards the thumb.

- Extend the wrist and draw the fingers in to form a fist, then extend the fingers again and place the hand flat on the table.

Finger exercises

- First place the forearm and the back of the hand on the table and bend the top and middle joints of the fingers, keeping the proximal joints straight. Then form a fist by bending all the joints of the fingers, with the thumb alternately inside and outside the fist. Then open the fist up again and straighten the fingers.

- Place the forearm and the palm of the hand flat on the table, slightly incline the hand from the wrist in the direction of the little finger and then move each finger in turn back towards the thumb, without moving the wrist.

Thumb exercises

- Extend the thumb away from the index finger and flex the muscles vigorously, repeating the exercise several times.

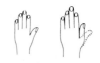

- Clasp your hands, enclosing one of your thumbs so that only its top joint is free. Bend and stretch this joint vigorously. Clasp the hands so that the left and right thumbs are enclosed alternately.

- Move the top joint of the thumb across the palm, making contact with each of the finger tips in turn. During this exercise, all the finger joints should be bent.

Changes in the nape of the neck in inflammatory diseases of the joints

Where pain, restricted movement, tension or other difficulties are experienced in the vicinity of the neck vertebrae and the adjacent muscles and tissues, it is essential to consult a doctor, physiotherapist or ergotherapist as to the most suitable course of action, due to the complexity of the specific problems related to this area (see p.87–89).

Principal problems experienced

- Pain.

- Restricted movement.

- Reduced stability.

Relaxation of the neck

- Wear a suitable soft collar.

- Massage to loosen up the painful muscles.

- Easy chair with suitable support for the neck.

- Don't use the safety belt when driving! (It will be necessary to obtain legal exemption.)

Changes in the lower extremities in inflammatory diseases of the joints

(for anatomy, see Patient Instruction Sheet 1)

Pain

Restricted movement

Hips	The most common difficulties experienced are the inability to stretch the hip joints and restricted inward movement of the legs.
Knees	Frequently, it is impossible to stretch the knee fully.
Foot joints	When the lower leg is standing vertical, it is frequently impossible to lift the foot clear of the ground. This is known as footdrop or 'fixed plantar flexion'.
	The ankle often leans outwards when weight is put on it: pes valgus.
Toes	Frequently, the big toes are inclined towards the little toes (hallux valgus). The bottom and top joints of the big toes are often stiff, and possibly even angled upwards: this is known as hallux rigidus.
	In polyarthritis, the bottom joints of the little toes are generally overstretched, while the middle joints are locked in flexion: hammer toes.
	If the bottom joints are more or less in the neutral position, while the middle and top joints of the side toes are locked in pronounced flexion, this deformity is known as clawfoot.
	In chronic polyarthritis, the bottom joints of the toes are generally damaged by the inflammation. A considerable amount of horny skin and nodules (corns) can build up at

pressure points, and eventually lead to lesions. This is particularly the case where the skin under pressure is directly on top of the bone.

Leg length difference Differences in the lengths of the legs can lead to deformities in the joints which support the weight of the body. The results can take the form of a chain reaction (see sketch).

Weakness In most cases, the quadriceps muscle, or extensor muscle of the knee joint, is the first muscle to atrophy and show pronounced weakness. More rarely, or at a later stage, the extensor muscles of the hip may become atrophied and weakened, followed by the abductor muscles of the hips.

Possible ways of compensating for differences in the length of the legs.

Functional demands on the flexibility of the joints of the lower extremities

Sitting Depending on the height of the chair, this calls for bending at the hip and knee joints of 90°, and for 20° upwards flexing of the feet from the ankle joints.

Walking Calls for 70° flexing of the knees, 10° flexing at the hips and 15–20° upwards flexing of the feet from the ankle joints.

Negotiating stairs Calls for ca. 50° flexing at the hips, 90–100° bending at the knees and 15–20° upwards flexing of the feet from the ankle joints.

Joint protection and stress relief in the region of the lower extremities

How can deformities be avoided?

- Treat inflammation: with medicaments, local steroid injections, ankle supports, synovectomy of the knees, ankles or bottom joints of the toes.

- Contracture prophylaxis carried out in a relaxed state: physiotherapeutic exercises in a warm kinotherapeutic bath.

- Careful foot hygiene, thorough drying, possibly using a hair drier, after washing the feet or bathing, perfectly fitting shoes, good ventilation.

- Strengthening of the extensor muscles of the hips and knees, and of the abdominal muscles.

- Reduction of strain in the joints by:
  - Using walking aids specially adapted to the hand and arm functions.
  - Taking heed of pain, taking short breaks in a relaxed position.
  - Frequent changes of position when working.
  - Use of suitable implements and devices wherever possible, e.g. to raise the height of a chair to assist sitting down and standing up.
  - Descending stairs backwards if necessary.
  - Frequently lying face downwards, allowing the feet to hang down over the end of the bed, or on the back of a relatively firm flat couch.
  - Adapting your surroundings.

Contracture prophylaxis in the region of the lower extremities

Every joint should be exercised at least once a day. This should quickly become part of the daily routine. The exercises can be spaced out over the entire day. Each exercise should be carried out slowly and rhythmically, and pain should be avoided or circumvented. And don't forget to take rests in between! Many of the exercises can be carried out lying on a suitable couch or bed. The achievement of a sufficiently relaxed state can be assisted by controlled abdominal breathing.

Foot exercises

- Bend the feet upwards and downwards from the ankles, turn the toes under and stretch them again, rotate the feet and, if possible, spread the toes and bring them together again. These exercises should be repeated as often as possible.

Hips – Knees

- Draw the knee up, at the same time bending the hip as far as possible, allowing the heel to drag along the bed. Stretch the leg again, reversing the process. Exercise each leg separately.

- If one leg involuntarily follows the other during this exercise, seek the advice of a physiotherapist. The probable cause is flexion contracture in the hip in question.

- Lie on the back with the legs outstretched and slightly apart and turn the feet inwards and outwards.

- Stretch the thigh muscles as vigorously as possible, so that the knee joint is straightened. This is a particularly important exercise and should be repeated at frequent intervals throughout the day.

- Move the outstretched leg to the side without raising it. Exercise each leg separately.

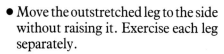

- Bend the knees and draw the feet up slightly, then lift the pelvis and stretch the buttock muscles vigorously.

Abdominal muscles

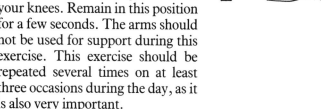

- Lie down with hips and knees bent and feet flat on the bed, and raise the head so that you have a good view of your knees. Remain in this position for a few seconds. The arms should not be used for support during this exercise. This exercise should be repeated several times on at least three occasions during the day, as it is also very important.

- Alternatively: if pain is experienced in the neck, the patient can lie flat with knees drawn up and press down on to the bed with the back and arms, draw in the stomach and remain in this position for about 10 seconds. Rest a while and then repeat.

After Althoff and Nordenskiöld (1985).

Organisation of household and domestic arrangements

The aids available to the arthritis sufferer are nowadays so many and varied that for most patients suffering from chronic polyarthritis, housework can be made very much easier. However, a number of basic rules must be observed:

- The family and other members of the household must be involved in the household chores.

- The individual jobs must be stripped to their bare essentials.

- There are always more unnecessary steps to any job than one would ever think possible.

- Give up any idea of striving for perfection: too many rheumatic patients demand too much of themselves.

In the kitchen, in particular, one should start by going through the larder and the storage cupboards and removing anything that is not used at least once a year. Implements and utensils should be kept as near as possible to the spot where they are needed. Go out and buy lightweight pots and pans, crockery and essential tools, unless these are already available. Utensils that are used at the same time should be kept together in the same place, e.g.:

Crockery racks, kitchen towels, detergents	by the sink
Bread board, bread knife or slicer	by the bread bin
Coffee pot, coffee, filters, oven gloves	by the stove

The kitchen should be equipped as a pleasant and functional place of work, not like an exhibition stand.

Simplify the household laundering:

- Buy non-iron clothes where possible.

- If you don't wish to give up ironing altogether, use a lightweight iron. Seek the advice of a physiotherapist or ergotherapist as to what type of chair to use in the kitchen, and try it out.

A good vacuum cleaner is essential. Castors on heavy pieces of furniture can be a godsend. If the patient has difficulties with the hands, a suitable orthopaedic splint can be fitted. Many jobs can simply be delegated to other members of the family or voluntary helpers. On the whole, cleaning and dusting should not be overdone. The patient should always allow plenty of time to rest between jobs. As a polyarthritis sufferer, both you and your family have much to gain by not overdoing things.

Going out to work

For many arthritis sufferers, the ability to continue going out to work as before, or to train for some other less exacting work, either full-time or part-time, provides an enormous incentive to keep going. In such cases, one should have no qualms about assigning a lower priority to the household chores. However, one should also consider the following:

- Travelling backwards and forwards between the home and one's place of work should be as comfortable and stress-free as possible.

- The normal measures taken to protect the joints at home should also be taken at the place of work.

- A visit by an ergotherapist or physiotherapist familiar with the nature of one's work is necessary to discuss possible ways of taking the physical effort out of it, in order to protect the joints and tendons.

- Check whether there are any public (or private) bodies in the country who are prepared to give financial assistance to help with travel, retraining, etc.

General guidelines for the use of medicaments

- Unless express instructions to the contrary are given by the doctor, all medications should be taken with food or drink (milk, water).

- Never take more than the dose prescribed by the doctor. Many medicaments are prescribed individually. Children, in particular, will be prescribed lower dosages. These are usually calculated according to their body weight.

- All medicaments should be stored in a safe place, well out of the reach of children.

- The doctor treating or monitoring the condition of the arthritis patient should be informed of any other treatment or medicaments the patient is receiving from another doctor for any other condition. Some medicaments show a favourable or unfavourable reaction if taken at the same time as other medicaments (drug interaction).

- Certain preparations must not be taken during pregnancy. If a pregnancy is planned, then the doctor treating the patient should be consulted at once.

- The patient should always read the slip enclosed with the medicament very carefully. If there are any points requiring clarification, these should be discussed with the doctor in charge at the earliest opportunity.

So-called symptomatic medicaments (analgesics and anti-inflammatory drugs)

Salicylates

- In small doses, salicylate preparations can have an analgesic effect; in larger doses, i.e. ca. 4 g or more per day in total, they can also have an anti-inflammatory effect.

- Side-effects: gastric disorders, gastric haemorrhages (generally only microscopic), ringing in the ears, dizziness, retarded coagulation of the blood.

Indomethacin

- Powerful anti-inflammatory drug, eases stiffness and painful joints; in capsules of 25 mg or 50 mg, slow-release capsules of 75 mg, suppositories of 100 mg.

- Suppositories are mainly administered at night to ease pain and combat morning stiffness (generally with success). The drug also has a sedative effect and thus helps the patient sleep.

- Guide to average dosage: as a rule, 200 mg is regarded as the maximum total daily dose (24 hours).

- Side-effects: nausea, headaches, dizziness, gastric disorders. Occasionally, gastric haemorrhages. If possible, this preparation should not be taken by patients who have already had a gastric or duodenal ulcer.

Naproxen

- An effective anti-inflammatory and analgesic drug for use in treating patients with diseases of the joints.
  Few side-effects, none of them dangerous.

- Guide to average dosage: 250 mg morning and evening, possibly 500 mg at night.

Ibuprofen

- Also a very effective anti-inflammatory preparation which is particularly good for stiffness and pain.
  Few side-effects, none of them dangerous.

- Guide to average dosage: 0.6 to 1.2 g daily in three or four divided doses.

Long-acting basic preparations

Anti-malarial drugs

- In many cases, these attenuate the inflammatory and destructive action of the rheumatic disease and in time lead to a decrease in joint tenderness and pain and a lowering of blood sedimentation rate.

- The full effects can only be measured after a long period of administration (4–6 months).

- In Sweden, interruption of the treatment for a period of 8–12 weeks is recommended once a year. This is usually during the summer months.

- Chloroquine may not be taken during pregnancy, or if the patient is also suffering from psoriasis.

- Guide to average dosage: chloroquine 150 mg, 1 tablet per day.

- Side-effects: at the recommended dose, disturbed vision, sleeplessness, loss of appetite, dizziness and slight irritability may occur on very rare occasions. These side-effects are not dangerous.

- Long-term side-effects: hair grows lighter in colour, skin becomes more sensitive to direct sunlight. No sunbathing! Wear sunglasses! Where the eyes are affected, slight traces of chloroquine may appear on the cornea and retina. Before medication commences, it is essential to consult an eye specialist, who should also check the eyes every six months while the treatment is in progress. Retinal changes and corneal opacities are an indication to stop medication.

Gold and penicillamine
Both these preparations can also have a suppressive effect on the inflammatory and destructive activity which occurs in chronic polyarthritis and also in juvenile chronic polyarthritis. Their effect, too, does not become apparent for a period of 6–12 months. Where correctly indicated, use of one of these medicaments is strongly recommended, though due to the increased side-effects, regular checks by the doctor, including a standard laboratory test, are necessary. Patients whose doctor prescribes one of these medicaments should ask him for detailed information.

Immunosuppressants and cytostatic agents
These preparations are used if the disease takes a more active and aggressive form and the above-mentioned three basic preparations have little or no effect. These preparations have certain side-effects which necessitate careful analysis of the blood and urine at frequent intervals. Here again, patients must seek detailed individual advice from their doctor.

Corticosteroids (hormone preparations)
These preparations are derived from the hormone cortisone, which is produced in the body by the suprarenal cortex. They have a very

powerful anti-inflammatory effect, but like all other medications, they have no direct influence on the actual course of the disease.

- If the patient has to consult another doctor for some other complaint, then it is absolutely essential to inform him that steroids are being, or have been taken, and in what quantities. This is particularly important in the case of infectious diseases, or with any type of surgical intervention.

- Corticosteroid preparations may not be suddenly discontinued. The dose must be reduced extremely slowly and under strict medical supervision.

- Present-day corticosteroid preparations have only a fraction of the side-effects of the original cortisone. Usually prednisone or prednisolone in table form is prescribed nowadays.

- As a rule, the average dosage of these is 2.5, 5 or 7.5 mg per day, where possible only for a very short period of time. The total daily dose is taken in the morning. Usually, with a daily dose of less than 5 mg, the body's own production of cortisone is hardly affected. In most cases, however, the long-term therapeutic effect of such a dose is too small. Certain cytostatic agents, e.g. azathioprine, which are very effective when used as basic preparations and rarely cause side-effects, enable the daily dose of prednisone or predniso-lone to be reduced slowly a milligram at a time after 6–12 months.

- The corticosteroid preparations have a pronounced, and initially often astonishing, analgesic effect, either as a result of their powerful anti-inflammatory action or by directly influencing the patient's perception of the pain.

- Side-effects: marked improvement in general well-being, positive frame of mind, gastric disorders, occasional gastric haemorrhages, varying degrees of bone atrophy, harmless bruising under the skin, increased susceptibility to infectious diseases, impaired hormone production, increased coagulability, occasionally high blood pressure. Particular care should be taken when prescribing corticosteroid preparations for polyarthritis patients with high blood pressure or diabetes or who have had gastric or duodenal ulcers.

Local corticosteroid treatment

- Modified corticosteroid preparations can be injected or infiltrated directly into the joints, tendon attachments, tendon sheaths and synovial bursae. Locally, the anti-inflammatory effect is very pronounced, pain and swelling recede very quickly, but usually only temporarily. The duration of this effect varies.

- Side-effects: local disappearance of fatty tissue, muscle or tendon fibres.

- Contraindications: infected wounds.

- Caution! Local steroid treatment may only be carried out under special aseptic or antiseptic conditions. It represents an essentially short-term solution to a local problem (Dixon 1983).

Social problems with chronic polyarthritis

Adapting the home

The following changes are often necessary: replacing the bath with a shower, changing the taps and installing single-handed mixer taps, removing all the door sills. It is worth investigating to what extent local authorities and other public bodies can render financial assistance with such changes.

Place of work

The arthritis sufferer's place of work should be analysed to determine whether it is suitable as it is, or whether it can be adapted to meet the particular requirements of the arthritis sufferer. A reduction in working hours could be considered, with the loss of earnings hopefully being made good through social security. In other cases, it may be necessary to think in terms of retraining for a physically less demanding occupation (see p.228).

Financial assistance

Sickness benefits and other social security benefits are handled differently from one country to another and from one insurer to another. There may, for example, be state pensions payable for partial or complete premature retirement due to invalidity. The same applies to payments designed to assist retraining, to provide special aids, transport such as wheelchairs, electric wheelchairs, specially adapted cars, and also for helpers. As a general rule, it is important that contact should be made with the appropriate social workers, through the doctor or physiotherapist or ergotherapist. If there are any specialist organisations concerned with rheumatism, or regional or national Rheumatism Associations, then it would be a good idea to approach these directly. Otherwise, advice should be sought from the local authorities, or Citizens Advice Bureaux, etc.

In some places, there are self-help organisations set up by and for polyarthritis or ankylosing spondylitis sufferers.

Glossary of technical terms

Abduct	To move outwards, away from body.
Acromioclavicular joint	Joint situated between a prominence of the shoulder bone which serves as the roof of the shoulder joint and the collar bone, i.e. a lateral joint of the collar bone.
Active mobility	Movements of a joint which the patient can carry out independently.
Active period of the disease	Period in which the inflammation flares up, the joints become swollen, over-heated and especially painful.
Adduct	To move inwards, towards the body.
Ankylosing spondylitis	Bechterew's disease, rheumatism of the spine with a strong tendency to stiffening in the affected joints.
Arthrodesis	Stiffening of a joint.
Arthroplasty	Surgical replacement of a joint with a prosthesis.
Carpal tunnel	Channel in the wrist on the palm side. The floor and side walls are provided by wrist bones, while the ceiling of the tunnel is provided by the thick, inelastic volar transverse ligament. The walls of the tunnel are therefore unable to yield. The nine long flexor tendons of the fingers together with their sheaths and the median nerve run through this tunnel from the forearm to the hand.
Carpal tunnel syndrome	Pressure from the surrounding structures or from the swollen tendons or tendon sheaths on the median nerve in the tunnel. This pressure leads to tingling, pain and disorders of sensation in the first four fingers, leading eventually to muscular atrophy in the ball of the thumb.

Carpus	Wrist
Contracture	Non-correctable deformity of a joint, caused by shortening of the corresponding muscles, tendons or sections of the capsule.
Contracture prophylaxis	Preventive treatment to prevent the formation of deformities in the joints as a result of shortening of the muscles and tendons or the destruction of the stabilising soft parts or the joint cartilage and sections of bone close to the joint.
Differences in lengths of leg –	
actual	The skeleton of the leg is shorter on one side than on the other.
functional	The leg on one side appears to be longer or shorter than on the other. The reason for this apparent difference is a deformity of the back, or in the hip or knee.
DIP joints	Distal interphalangeal joints = top joints of the fingers.
Dorsal	Pertaining to the back, the back of the hand or of the foot or situated on the side of the back, or the back of the hand or foot.
Dorsal side	The rear surface of the hand, the foot or the torso.
Exudate	Inflammatory fluid in a joint.
Extension	Movement bringing the members of a limb into or towards a straight condition.
Extensor	Any muscle that extends a joint.
Femur	Thigh bone.
Flexion	The act of bending or the condition of being bent.
Flexor	Any muscle that bends a joint.
Functional analysis	Careful examination, including tests, to determine to what extent the hands, arms, feet, legs,

236

spine, etc. can fulfil the requirements of every-day life.

Hip extensors	The extensor muscles of the hip, consisting mainly of the gluteal muscles.
Humeroscapular joint	Joint between the socket at the lateral termination of the shoulder blade and the head of the humerus.
Hyperextension	Extension beyond the normal limit.
Inactive period of the disease	Period during the course of chronic poly-arthritis which is largely or completely free from inflammation. During this period, the joints are not swollen or over-heated, and are less painful or even free from pain. At this time, the patients also feel less tired.
IP joints	Interphalangeal joints = the two outer finger joints.
Joint status	Record of the state of the joints, with particular reference to temperature, swelling, stability, appearance, mobility, pain on movement, end phase pain, pain at rest, etc.
Kyphosis	Abnormally increased convexity in the curvature of the thoracic spine, as in hunchback.
Lordosis	Forward curvature of the lumbar spine.
Luxation	Condition in which the surfaces of the joint have slipped so far relative to one another that they have lost contact, and the function of the joint is seriously affected.
MCP joints	Metacarpophalangeal joints = bottom joints of the fingers, between the metacarpal bones and the bottom phalanges of the fingers.
Orthoplast	Thermoplastic material used for individual shaping of collars and immobilisation splints, cf. also Plastazote.
Orthosis	Splint
Passive mobility	Movement in a joint produced by another person.

PIP joints	Proximal interphalangeal joints = middle joints of the fingers.
Planta pedis	Sole of the feet.
Plantar	Pertaining to the sole.
Plastazote	Thermoplastic material used for individual shaping of collars and immobilisation splints, cf. also Orthoplast.
Progression	Advance, deterioration or increasing spread of a disease or process.
Pronation	Turning the palm inwards and backwards when the arm is hanging down, turning the palm downwards when the forearm is horizontal.
Pronate	To subject to pronation.
Quadriceps	Four-headed muscle on the front of the thigh which bends the hip and straightens the knee.
Radial	On the forearm, on the side of the radius or the thumb.
Radius	The forearm bone.
Remission	Period in which the disease is inactive.
Resection	Surgical removal of tissue.
Sacro-iliac joint	Joint between the sacrum and the ilium.
Scoliosis	Lateral deviation in the normally straight vertical line of the spine.
Subluxation	The surfaces of the joint have slipped relative to one another and have partially lost contact with one another. The joint is only partially functional, and the surface actually loaded is much reduced in size.
Supination	Turning the palm forward when the arm is hanging down, turning the palm upwards when the forearm is held horizontal.
Supinate	To subject to supination.

238

Suspension	Supporting of individual limbs from above to relieve stress or alleviate inflammation.
Synovectomy	Removal of the inflamed inner layer of the joint capsule.
Synovia	Joint lubricating fluid.
Synovial fluid	Joint fluid (synovia).
Synovial membrane	Inner layer of joint capsule.
Tendinitis	Inflammation of tendon and tendon–muscle attachments.
Tendon rupture	Tearing of a tendon.
Tenosynovitis	Inflammation of the tendon sheaths.
Thorax	Thoracic cage.
Tibia	Shin bone.
Traction treatment	Exertion of a pulling force to stretch a joint in the longitudinal axis.
Ulna	Lateral forearm bone.
Ulnar	Pertaining to the ulna, the side of the forearm and hand with the ulna and little finger.
Ulnar deviation	Angling of the fingers from the bottom joints in the direction of the ulnar side.
Ulnar drift	Ulnar deviation.
Valgus position	Deformity characterised by knock-knees. The joint forms an open angle to the side.
Valgus position of the foot	Pes valgus.
Varus position	Deformity characterised by bow-legs. The joint forms an open angle to the inside.
Volar	On the side of the palm.
Volar subluxation	Slipping of the surfaces of the bottom finger joints in the direction of the palm, with partial loss of contact with the head of the metacarpal bones.

BIBLIOGRAPHY

The reader will find here the original literature used by the authoress, which consists of books, papers and references in Swedish and English, except for one book, by C. Tillmann, on the rheumatic foot in German.

ALLANDER, E (1970): A population survey of rheumatoid arthritis. Epidemiological aspects of the syndrome, its pattern and effect on gainful employment. Acta Rheum Scand, Suppl 15.

ALTHOFF, B (1973): Ny reumatikerkäpp. Sjukgymnasten *11*: 1–3.

ALTHOFF, B and GOLDIE, J (1980): Cervical collars in atlanto-axial subluxation, a radiographic comparison. Ann Rheum Dis *39*: 485-489.

ALTHOFF, B and NORDENSKIÖLD, U (1977): Ledskydd ett skonsamt levnadssätt. Riksförbundet mot Reumatism.

ALTHOFF, B and NORDENSKIÖLD, U (1985):Joint protection. An alleviating way of living. Pharmacia, Uppsala.

AMERICAN ACADEMY OF ORTHOPEDIC SURGEONS: Joint motion. Method of measuring and recording. American Academy of Orthopedic Surgeons, 29 East Madison Street, Chicago, Illinois 60602.

ANDRÉN, E and NORDENSKIÖLD, U (1976): Emg-studie av m ext c ulnaris hos personer med reumatoid artrit. Stencil. Medicinsk rehabilitering 1, Sahlgrenska sjukhuset, Göteborg.

ANSELL, B M (1980): Rheumatic Disorders in Childhood. Butterworth, London, Boston, Sydney, Wellington, Durban, Toronto.

AWERBUCH, M S, HENDERSON, D R F, MILAZZO, S C, WHITE, R G, and UTTERKAR, A B (1981): Long-term follow-up of posterior cervical fusion for atlanto-axial subluxation in rheumatoid arthritis. J Rheumatol *8*: 423-432.

BAKER, G H B (1981): Psychological management. Clin Rheum Dis 7: 455-469.

BALDURSSON, H and BRATTSTRÖM, H (1979): Sexual difficulties and total hip replacement in rheumatoid arthritis. Scand J Rheumatol *8*: 214–216.

BAUER, G (1979): Kirurgi 3 – ortopedi. Studentlitteratur.

BAUM, J (1982): A review of the psychological aspects of rheumatic diseases. Sem Arthritis Rheum *11*: 352-361.

BELCON, M C, HAYNES, R B and TUGWELL, P (1984): A critical review of compliance studies in rheumatoid arthritis. Arthritis Rheum *27*(11):1227-1233.

BENKTZON, M (1975): The development of kitchen tools and hand-grips based upon criteria for the handicapped. The Ninth ICSD Congress, Moscow.

BENKTZON, M (1982): Design for the disabled. Symposium on Scandinavian Design Now. New York.

BENKTZON, M and JUHLIN, S E (1984): Role of design. Design News *162-163*:16-17.

BENKTZON, M and JUHLIN, S E (1978): Utveckling av matberedningskärl för personer med nedsatt hand-armfunktion. STU-rapport 77:3551.

BENKTZON, M and JUHLIN, S E (1978): Utveckling av äta-dricka-redskap. Slutrapport. Ergonomi Design AB.

BERGLUND, K (1975): Vägar mot mänskligare sjukvard. Läkartidningen *72*:4686–4689.

BERGLUND, K (1979): Inflammatoriska reumatiska sjukdomar – en inledning. Studentlitteratur.

BLOUNT, W P (1965): Don't throw away the cane. J. Bone Joint Surg *38A*:695–708.

BOGGS, J A (1977): Living and loving with arthritis. Socializing with the opposite. Honolulu, Hawaii.

BRATTSTRÖM, H and BRATTSTRÖM, M (1971): Long term results in knee arthrodesis in rheumatoid arthritis. Reconstr Surg Traumat *12*:125–137.

BRATTSTRÖM, H and GRANHOLM, L (1976): Atlanto-axial fusion in rheumatoid arthritis. Acta Orthop Scand *47*:619–628.

BRATTSTRÖM, H and KHUDIARY, H (1975): Synovectomy of the elbow in rheumatoid arthritis. Acta orthop Scan *46*:744–750.

BRATTSTRÖM, H and MORITZ, U (1971): Behandling av knäledskontrakturer. Läkartidningen *68*:5591–5596.

BRATTSTRÖM, H, JUNERFÄLT, I and MORITZ, U (1971): Kontraktur eller fraktur? Läkartidningen *68*: 304–306.

BRATTSTRÖM, M (1974*a*): New walking aids for rheumatic patients. Scan J Rehab Med 6:141–143.

BRATTSTRÖM, M (1974*b*): Sexuella problem vid ledsjukdomar. I Sex och Handikapp. SVCRS Skriftserie nr 15.

BRATTSTRÖM, M (1975): Teamwork in the rehabilitation of patients with chronic rheumatic disease. Ann Clin Research 7:230–236.

BRATTSTRÖM, M (1977): The rheumatism dispensary in specialized outpatient care of rheumatic patients. Läkartidningen *74*:4501–4503.

BRATTSTRÖM, M and BERGLUND, K (1970): Ambulant rehabilitation of patients with chronic rheumatic disease. Scan J Rehab Med *2*:133–142.

BRATTSTRÖM, M and LARSSON, B M (1983). The arthritic at work. International Rehabilitation Research 6(1): 79-81.

BRATTSTRÖM, M and SUNDBERG, J (1965): Juvenile rheumatoid gonarthritis. I. Clinical and roentgenological study. II. Disturbance of ossification and growth. Acta rheum Scand *11*:266–290.

BRATTSTRÖM, M, BRAFELT, I. HEMMINGSSON, I B and PAULSSON, K (1977): Varför blir reumatiker rullstolsanvändare. Information fran PTI (Psykotekniska Institutet) nr 92.

BRATTSTRÖM, M, BRATTSTRÖM, H, EKLÖF, M and FREDSTRÖM, J (1981): The rheumatoid patient in need of a wheelchair. Scan J Rehab Med *13*:39–43.

BRATTSTRÖM, M, EKLÖF, M, MALCUS, P and CLAESSON, K (1980): The instruction of patients at the rheumatism dispensary in Lund. *Läkartidningen* 77:3509.

BREWERTON, D A and LETTIN, A W F (1974): The rheumatoid hand and its management. *In* Rehabilitation of the Hand (ed. C B Wynn Parry), Butterworth.

BREWERTON, D A, CAFFREY, M, HART, F *et al.* (1973): Ankylosing spondylitis and HL, A-B 27. Lancet *I*:904–907.

BRUNNSTRÖM, S (1966): Clinical kinesiology. 2nd edition. F A Davis.

BÄCKDAHL, M (1963): The caput ulnae syndrome in rheumatoid arthritis. Acta Rheum Scan, Suppl 5.

CAILLIET, R (1967): Shoulder pain. F A Davis Company.

CAILLIET, R (1968): Foot and ankle pain. F A Davis Company

CAILLIET, R (1973): Knee pain and disability. F A Davis Company

CAILLIET, R (1975): Hand pain and impairment. F A Davis Company

CHAMBERLAIN, A (1984): Joint protection. Clin Rheum Dis *10*:727-743.

CHAMBERLAIN, A (1977): Social implications of rheumatoid arthritis in young mothers. Pers Comm, San Francisco.

CHAMBERLAIN, A and BUCHANAN, J M (1977): Survey of the mobility of the disabled in an urban environment. The Royal Association for Disability and Rehabilitation.

CHAMBERLAIN, MA (1983): Socioeconomic effects of ankylosing spondylitis in females: a comparison of 25 female with 25 male subjects. Int Rehabil Med 5(3):149-153.

CHAO, E Y, OPGRANDE J D and AXMEAR, F E (1976): Three dimensional forces analysis of finger joints in selected isometric hand functions. J Biomechanics 9: 387–396.

CHUSID, G and McDONALD, J J (1970): Correlative neuroanatomy and functional neurology. Lange Medical Publications, Los Altos, California.

CORDERY, J C (1962): Conservation of physical resources in the activities of patients with arthritis and connective tissue disorders. Study Course III. World Federation Occupational Therapists. Third International Congress 1962.

CORDERY, J C (1965): Joint protection: A responsibility of the occupational therapist. Amer J Occup Therapy *19*:5.

CULLBERG, J (1976): Kris och utveckling. Natur och Kultur.

CURREY, H L F (1970): Osteoarthritis of the hip joint and sexual activity. Ann Rheum Dis *29*:488.

DEANE, G (1970): Some biomechanical considerations in hip and knee surgery. Clinics in Rheumatic Diseases *4*:327–346.

DEAVER, G G (1966): Crutches, braces, canes and walkers. Rehab. Monograph XXX. Inst of Rehab Med, New York University Medical Center, 400 East 34th Street, N.Y. 10016.

DEL BUENO, D J (1978): Patient education planning for success. Journal of Nursing Administration, pp.3–7, (June).

DIXON, A and GRABER, J (1983): Local injection therapy in rheumatic diseases. Eular Monograph Series No.4.

DIXON, A and KATES, A (1970): The rheumatoid foot. Proc Roy Soc Med *63*:1–4.

EBERHARDT, H D and INMAN, V T (1966): Fundamental studies of human locomotion. *In* Clinical Kinesiology (ed. S Brunnström), 2nd edition. F A Davis Company, Philadelphia.

EDSTRÖM, L and NORDEMAR, R (1974): Differential changes in type I and type II muscle fibres in rheumatoid arthritis. Scan J Rheumatol *3*:155–160.

ELLIS, M (1984): Splinting the rheumatoid hand. Clin Rheum Dis *10*:673–697.

ELST, P, SYBESMA, T, van der STADT, RJ, PRINS, AP, MULLER, WH and den BUTTER, A (1984): Sexual problems in rheumatoid arthritis and ankylosing spondylitis. Arthritis Rheum *27*(2):217–220.

ERLICH, G (1973*a*): Sexual problems of arthritic patient. *In* Total Management of the Arthritic Patient. J B Lippincott Co, Philadelphia.

ERLICH, G (1973*b*): *In* Total Management of the Arthritic Patient. J B Lippincott Co, Philadelphia.

ELLIS, M I, SEDHOM, B B, AMIS, A A, DOWSON, D and WRIGHT, V (1979): Forces in the knee joint while rising from normal and motorized chairs. Engineering in Medicine *8*:33–40.

ENGLISH, C B and NALEBUFF, E A (1971): Understanding the arthritic hand. Amer J Occup Therapy *25*:352–359.

FEARNLEY, G R (1952): Ulnar Deviation of the Fingers. Ann Rheum Dis *11*:219.

FEINBERG, JR and BRANDT, KD (1984): Allied health team management of rheumatoid arthritis patients. Am J Occup Ther *38*(9):613–620.

FLATT, A I (1968): *In* The Care of the Rheumatoid Hand. 2nd edition. C V Mosby Company, St Louis.

FRANKEL, V H and NORDIN, M (1980): Basic biomechanics of the skeletal system. Lea and Febiger, Philadelphia.

FRIES, JF et al. (1980): Measurement of patient outcome in arthritis. Arthritis Rheum *23*:137–146.

FREDIN, B (1977): Att vara reumatiker. Läkartidningen 74:4520–4521.

GIGT og Hverdag (1972): Rigsforeningen til Gigtens Bekaempelse, Copenhagen.

GOLDIE, I (1975): Lateral release and capsulotomy. An operative procedure in the treatment of flexion contracture of the rheumatoid knee joint. Acta Orthop Belgica *41*:606–618.

GREENGROSS, W (1974): Marriage, sex and arthritis. Arthritis and Rheum.

GREENGROSS, W (1976): Entitled to love. Malaby Press Limited, London.

GRIMBY, G (1977): Muskelkraft – mätmetodik och träningseffekter. Ur Aktuellt om muskelträning. Läkartidningen *74*:3891–3893.

GANGHJÄLPMEDEL. Rapport Handikappinstitutet 3/1976.

HAGERT, C G (1978): Advances in hand surgery. Finger joint implants. Surgery Annual *10*: 253–275.

HAMILTON, A (1981): Sexual problems in arthritis and allied conditions. International Rehabilitation Medicine *3*:38.

HAZLEMAN, B L and WATSON, P G (1977): Ocular implications of rheumatoid arthritis. Clin Rheum Dis *3*:510–526.

HELAL, B (1984): The flexor tendon apparatus in the rheumatoid hand. Clin Rheum Dis *10*:479–501.

HERAMB, K (1982): Handicappedes sexuella problemer. Ugeskrift for praktisk laegegerning.

HJORTH, L and VINTERBERG, H (1981): Gruppendervisning af patienter med arthritis rheumatoides Ugeskr Laeger *141*:1595–1598.

HOLLANDER, J L (1979): Arthritis and allied conditions. Lea & Febiger, Philadelphia.

HUSKISSON, E C (1976): Assessment for clinical trials. Clin Rheum Dis *2*:37–49.

INMAN, V T (1947): Functional aspects of the abductor muscles of the hip. J Bone Joint Surg *29*:607–619.

INMAN, V T, SAUNDERS, J B M and ABBOTT, L C (1944): Observations on the function of the shoulder joint. J Bone Joint Surg (Amer) *26*:1–30.

ISENBERG, D (1984): Inflammatory disorders of muscle. Clin Rheum Dis *10*:151–174.

JACOBY, R K, VIDIGAL, E, KIRKUP, J and DIXON A St (1976): The great toe as a clinical problem in rheumatoid arthritis. Rheumatology and Rehabilitation *15*:143–147.

JANSEN, B, LINDELÖF, I S and NILSSON, K (1976): Behov av psykologinsatser vid reumatiska sjukdomar. Umea Universitet. Psykolog. examensarbete 1976 (stencil).

KAIJ, L (1974): Den kroniskt sjuke patienten. Föreingen för psykisk hälsovard.

KAPLAN, S and KOZIN, F (1981): A controlled study of group counselling in rheumatoid arthritis. J Rheumatol *8*:91–99.

KATAOKA, O, HIROHATA, K and KURIHARA, A (1979): The surgical treatment of myelopathy secondary to rheumatoid arthritis of the lower cervical spine. Int Orthopaedics (SICOT) 3:103-110.

KATZ, S, DOWNS, T D and CASH, H R (1970): Progress in development of index of ADL. Gerontologist 10:20–30.

KATZ, S, FORD A, MOSKOWITZ, R and JACKSON, B (1963): Studies of illness in the aged: the index of ADL. A standardized measure of biological and psychosocial function. JAMA 185:914–919.

KATZ, S, VIGNOS, P J Jr, MOSKOWITZ, R W, THOMPSON, H M and SVEC, K H (1968): Comprehensive outpatient care in rheumatoid arthritis: a controlled study. JAMA 206:1244.

KAUFMAN, R L and GLENN, W V Jr (1983): Rheumatoid cervical myelopathy: evaluation by computerized tomography with multiplanar reconstruction. J Rheumatol 10:42–54.

KAY, A, DAVISON, B, BADLEY, E and WAGSTAFF, S (1983): Hip arthroplasty: patient satisfaction. Br J Rheumatol 22(4):243–249.

KELLY et al. (1984): Textbook of rheumatology. Philadelphia: WB Saunders.

KIRKUP, J R, VIDIGAL, E and JACOBY, R K (1977): The hallux and rheumatoid arthritis. Acta Orthop Scand 48:527–544.

KIRKUP, J R (1974): Ankle and tarsal joints in rheumatoid arthritis. Scand J Rheumatol 3:50–52.

KIVINIEMI, P (1977): Emotions and personality in rheumatoid arthritis. Scand J Rheumatol, suppl. 18.

KNOTT, M (1964): Neuromuscular facilitation in the treatment of rheumatoid arthritis. J Am Phys Ther 44:737.

LANNEFELT, K J (1969): Self-help manual for arthritis patients. Arthritis foundation, 475 Riverside Drive, New York 10027.

LANSBURY, I (1966): Methods for evaluating rheumatoid arthritis. In: Hollander, J L, ed. Arthritis and allied conditions. Lea and Febiger.

LEE, P, JASANI, M K, DICK, W C and BUCHANAN, E (1973): Evaluation of functional index in rheumatoid arthritis. Scand J Rheumatol 2:71-77.

LIANG, M H and JETTE A M (1981): Measuring functional ability in chronic arthritis. A critical review. Arthritis Rheum 24:80.

LUNDBLAHD, K and SVENSSON, B (1971): Blankett för utprovning av rullstol. Sjukgymnasten 9/1971.

McEWAN, C (1971): Ankylosing spondylitis and spondylitis accompanying ulcerative colitis, regional enteritis, psoriasis and Reiter's disease. Arthur Rheum 14:291.

MAHONEY, F I and BARTHEL D W (1965): Functional Evaluation: The Barthel Index. Maryland State Medical Journal 24:61–65.

MANNERFELT, L (1966): Studies on the hand in ulnar nerve paralysis. Acta Orthop Scand, Suppl 87.

MANNERFELT, L (1966): Studies on the hand in ulnar nerve paralysis. Acta Orthop scand, Suppl 87.

MANNERFELT, L and NORMAN, O: (1969) Attrition ruptures of flexor tendons in rheumatoid arthritis caused by bony spurs in the carpal tunnel. A clinical and radiological study. J Bone Joint Surg *51B:270 – 277*.

MARKS, J S and SHARP, J (1981): Rheumatoid cervical myelopathy. Q J Med, New series L *199*:307-319.

MARTEL, W (1961): The occipito-atlanto-axial joints in rheumatoid arthritis and ankylosing spondylitis. Amer J Roentgenol Radium Ther Nucl Med 86:223–240.

MATTHEWS, J A (1974): Atlantoaxial subluxation in rheumatoid arthritis. Ann Rheum Dis *33*:526–531.

MEARES, A (1971): Avspänd ùtan mediciner. Relief without drugs. Centraltryckeriet AB, Boras.

MEENAN, R et al (1980): Measuring health status in arthritis (AIMS). Arthritis Rheum *23*:146–152.

MELVIN, R F (1977): Rheumatic disease, occupational therapy and rehabilitation. F A Davis Company, Philadelphia.

MIKULOWSKI, P (1979): Dislokationsutveckling i occipitoaxiala regionen vid reumatoid artrit. Läkartidningen 76:300–304.

MIKULOWSKI, P, WOLLHEIM, F A, ROTMIL, P and OLSEN, I (1975): Sudden death in rheumatoid arthritis with atlanto-axial dislocation. Acta Med Scand *198*:445–451

MILLENDER, L H and NALEBUFF, E A (1973): Metacarpophalangeal joint arthroplasty utilizing the silicone rubber prostesis. Orthopedic Clin of North Amer *4*:349–371.

MILLENDER, L H and NALEBUFF, E A (1975): Preventive surgery, tenosynovectomy and synovectomy. Orthop Clin North Amer *6*:765–790.

MILLENDER, L H and NALEBUFF, E A (1975): Evaluation and treatment of early rheumatoid hand involvement. Orthop Clin North Amer 6:697–707.

MOBERG, E (1984): Splinting in hand therapy. New York: Thieme Stratton Inc.

MOLL, J M H (1980): Ankylosing spondylitis. Edinburgh: Churchill Livingstone.

MORITZ, U (1963): Electromyographic studies in adult rheumatoid arthritis. Acta rheum Scan, suppl 6:65.

MORITZ, U (1975): Nagra synpunkter pa övre extremitetens kinesiologi. Stencil SSGI.

MORITZ, U (1976): Nedsatt muskelfunktion vid reumatoid artrit. Sjukgymnasten *3*:4–5.

MORITZ, U (1976) Biomekaniska synpunkter pa muskelträning. Sjukgymnasten *3*:4–5.

MORITZ, U (1977): Biomekaniska synpunkter pa variationer i muskelstyrka. Ur Aktuellt om muskelträning. Läkaetidningen *74*:3892–3894.

MORITZ, U (1979): Measuring muscle strength. Scand J Rheum Supplement *30*, 66–67.

MORITZ, U and SVANTESSON, G (1970): Ganganalys i klinisk praxis. Stencil SSGI.

NALEBUFF, E A (1969): Diagnosis, classification and management of rheumatoid thumb deformities. Bull Hosp Joint Dis *29*:119–137.

NALEBUFF, E A (1975): The recognition and treatment of tendon ruptures in the rheumatoid hand. In: American Academy of Orthopaedic Surgeons Symposium on tendon surgery in the hand. St Louis: C V Mosby.

NALEBUFF, E A (1984): The rheumatoid thumb. Clin Rheum Dis *10*:589–608.

NALEBUFF, E A and MILLENDER, L H (1975): Surgical treatment of the swan neck deformity in rheumatoid arthritis. Orthop Clin North Amer 6:3, 733–752.

NALEBUFF, E A and POTTER, T A (1968): Rheumatoid involvement of tendons and tendon sheaths in the hand. Clin Orthop *59*:147–159.

NAPIER, J R (1956): The prehensile movements of the human hand. J Bone Joint Surg *38*:902–913.

NICHOLS, P J R (1971): Rehabilitation of the severly disabled: Wheelchairs, pp. 216–250, Butterworth.

NORDEMAR, R (1981): Physical training in rheumatoid arthritis. A controlled long-term study I–II. Scand J Rheumatol *10*:17–30.

NORDENSKIÖLD, U (1979): Ortosbehandling för händer. (Handikappinstitutet), Berlings, Lund. Tills m MOBERG, E, HAGERT, C G, SVENS, B & TRANEUS, M.

NORDISK LÄROBOK I REUMATOLOGI (1975): Almqvist & Wicksell.

NORDQVIST, I (1984): Sexual problems of physically disabled adolescents. SVCR, Stockholm.

OGRYZLO, M A (1972): Ankylosing spondylitis. *In* Arthritis and Allied Conditions (ed J L Hollander) pp. 699–721, Lea & Febiger.

ÖSTENSON, M and HUSBY,G (1983): A prospective clinical study of the effect of pregnancy on rheumatoid arthritis and ankylosing spondylitis. Arth Rheum 26(9).

OTTOSON, D and MYRENBERG, M (1975): Proprioceptive neuromuskulär faciliteringsbehandling. Svenska MS-föreningens riksförbund 1975.

PAHLE, J (1974): Skinner og Bandajer ved Ledelser i Overestremiteterne. Tekniske og ortopediske hjelpemidler for funksjonshemmede. Tanum, Oslo.

PAHLE, J and RAUNIO, P (1969): The influence of wrist position on finger deviation in the rheumatoid hand. J Bone Joint Surg *51B*:664.

PARKER, J C, SINGSEN, B H, HEWETT, J E, WALKER S E, HAZELWOOD, S E, HALL, P J, HOLSTEN, D J and RODON,C M (1984): Educating patients with rheumatoid arthritis: a prospective analysis. Arch Phys Med Rehabil 65:771–4.

PAULSSON, K BRAFELT, I and LUNDBLAD, B (1977): Rullstolsanvändarna i Gävleborgs län. Information fran PTI nr 91/1977.

PERRY, J (1967): Structural insufficiency. I. Pathomechanics, principles of lower extremity bracing. Phys Ther 47:848–852.

PERSELLIN, R H: The effect of pregnancy on rheumatoid arthritis. Bull Rheum Dis 27: 1976/77.

PERSSON, G (1975): Sträck – och benträningsapparat. Personal Communication. AB Rehabprodukter, Bokbindaregatan 3, 222 36 Lund.

PETTERSSON, C (1984): Studies on ageing and degeneration of the shoulder joint. Thesis, Malmö.

PINCUS et al (1983): Assessment of patient satisfaction in activities in daily living using a modified Stanforth health assessment questionnaire. Arth Rheum 26:1346–1353.

REDLUND JOHNELL, J (1984): Dislocations of the cervical spine in rheumatoid arthritis. Thesis, Malmö.

REKOLA, J K (1973): Rheumatoid arthritis and the family. Scan J Rheumatol 2, Suppl 3.

REZA, J M and VERITY, M A (1977): Neuromuscular manifestations of rheumatoid arthritis. Clin Rheum Dis 3:565–588.

RIMON, R (1969): A psychosomatic approach to rheumatoid arthritis. Acta Rheum Scand, Suppl 13.

RIMON, R and LAAKSO, R L (1984): Overt psychopathology in rheumatoid arthritis. A 15-year follow-up study. Scand J Rheumatol 13:324–328.

RITCHIE, D M, BOYLE, J A and McINNES, J M, et al.(1968): Clinical studies with an articular index for the assessment of joint tenderness in patients with rheumatoid arthritis. Quarterly J Med New Series 37:393–406.

ROBINSON, H and WALTERS, K (1979): Patterns of work – rheumatoid arthritis. Internat Rehab Med 1:121–125.

ROBINSON, H, KIRK, R F and FRYE, R L (1971): A psychological study of rheumatoid arthritis and selected controls. J Chron Dis 23:791–801.

ROOS, B, LYMARK, H and ANDERSON, L (1976): Technical aids for handicapped. A report on needs and goals. STU Information 18/1976.

RYDELL, N (1966): Forces in the hip joint. Part II: Intravital measurement. In Biomechanics and related bioengineering topics (ed. R M Kenedi), pp.351–357, Pergamon Press, Oxford.

SALTIN, B (1977): Människans skelett, muskelfibrer, egenskaper och funktion. Läkartidningen 74:3878–3883.

SCHOENING, H A (1965): Numerical scoring of self care status of patients. Arch Phys Med 46:689–697.

SHAPIRO, J S, HEIJMA, W, NASATIR, S and RAY, R D (1968): The relationship of wrist motion to ulnar phalangeal drift in the rheumatoid patient. Hand 3/1968

SIMON, L, BRUN, M and HOULEZ, G (1982): Polyarthrite rhumatoide et économie articulaire. Documenta Geigy.

SJÖLUND, A (1971): Gruppsykologi. Hallandspostens Boktryckeri, Halmstad.

SMITH, E M, JUVINALL, R C, BENDER, L F and PEARSON, J R (1964): Role of the finger flexors in rheumatoid deformities of the metacarpophalangeal joints. Arthur Rheum 7:467–490.

SMITH, E M, JUVINALL, R C, BENDER, L F and PEARSON, J R (1966): Flexor forces and rheumatoid metacarpophalangeal deformity. JAMA 198: 129–134.

SMITH, P, SHARP, J and BEUW, R T (1972): Natural history of rheumatoid cervical subluxations. Ann Rheum Dis 31:431–439.

SMITH, E M, JUVINALL, R C and CORELL, E B (1970): Bracing the unstable arthritis knee. Arch Phys Med Rehab 51:22.

SMYTHE, H A (1975): Assessment of joint disease. Toronto, January 1975 (Stencil).

SOLLERMANN, C and SPERLING, L (1977): Grip function of the healthy hand in a standardized hand function test. Scand J Rehab Med 9:123–129.

SOUTER, W (1979): Planning treatment of the rheumatoid hand. The Hand 1:3–16.

SPERLING, L (1979): Greppfunktion i dagligt liv. Studier över normala och funktionsnedsatta händer. Handikappforskningen. Göteborg.

STEINBROCKER, O, TRAEGER, C H and BATTERMAN, R C (1949): Therapeutic criteria in rheumatoid arthritis. JAMA 140:659.

STEWART, W F R (1975): Sex and physically handicapped. National Fund for Research into Crippling Deases. Vincent House, 1 Springfield Road, Horsham, Sussex, Sept. 1975.

SVANTESSON, H (1984): Barnreumatologi. Studentlitteratur, Lund.

SWANSON, A (1984): Postoperative care for patients with silastic finger joint implant. Michigan: Grand Rapids.

SWEZEY, R L: Dynamic factors in deformity of the rheumatoid arthritic hand. Bull Rheum Dis 22: 1971/72

SWEZEY, R (1978): Splints, braces, shoes and corsets. In Arthritis. Rational Therapy and Rehabilitation.

SWEZEY, R L (1978): Arthritis: Rational therapy and rehabilitation. Philadelphia.

SWEZEY, R L and SWEZEY, A (1976): Educational Theory as a basis for patient education. J. Chron Dis 29:417.

THORNELY, G, CHAMBERLAIN, A and WRIGHT, V (1977): Evaluation of aids and equipment for the bath and toilet. Occupational Therapy. University Department of Medicine, General Infirmary, Leeds.

THORSELL, U, BRATTSTRÖM, M and ÅHLUND, O (1984): Att bo och leva som rörelse-hindrad. 1. Reumatikers situation. Rapport R7. Lunds Universitet.

TILLMAN, K (1979): The rheumatoid foot. George Thieme Verlag.

TISELIUS, P (1969): Studies of joint temperature, joint stiffness and muscle weakness in rheumatoid arthritis. An experimental and clinical investigation. Acta Rheum Scan, Suppl 14.

VAUGHAN-JACKSON, O J (1958): Attrition ruptures of tendons in the rheumatoid hand. Proceedings of the Joint Meeting of the Orthopaedic Associations of the English Speaking World. J Bone Joint Surg *40A*:1431.

VIDIGAL, E, JACOBY, R K, DIXON, A St J, RATCLIFF, A H and KIRUP, I (1975): The foot in chronic rheumatoid arthritis. Ann Rheum Dis *34*: 292–297.

VIGNOS, P J, THOMSON, H M, KATZ, S, MOSKOWITZ, R W, FINK, S and SVEC, K H (1972): Comprehensive care and psychosocial factors in rehabilitation in chronic rheumatoid arthritis. A controlled study. J Chron Dis *457–467*.

VIGNOS, S, PARKER, W and THOMSON, H (1976): Evaluation of a clinical education programme for patients with rheumatoid arthritis. J Rheumatol *2*:155–156.

WIBERG, G (1975): Ortopedisk kirurgi. Studentlitteratur.

WILLIAMS, R C (1974): Rheumatoid arthritis as a systemic disease. Vol IV in the series: Major problems in Internal Medicine. W B Saunders Company, Philadelphia.

WILLIAMS, M and LISSNER, H R (1962): Biomechanics of human motion. W B Saunders Co, Philadelphia.

WRIGHT, V and OWEN, S (1976): The effect of rheumatoid arthritis on the social situation of housewives. Rheumatol Rehab *15*:155–160.

INDEX

255